HANDLEY PAGE

HASTINGS

Including
a brief history of the
Hermes

HANDLEY PAGE

HASTINGS

Including
a brief history of the
Hermes

TIM SENIOR

DALRYMPLE
& VERDUN◆
PUBLISHING

Hastings
Including a brief history of the Hermes
Tim Senior

ISBN 978-1-905414-07-9

First published in 2008 by
Dalrymple & Verdun Publishing
33 Adelaide Street, Stamford
Lincolnshire PE9 2EN
United Kingdom
Tel: 0845 838 1940
mail@dvpublishing.co.uk
www.dvpublishing.co.uk

© Concept and design
Dalrymple & Verdun Publishing and
Stephen Thompson Associates
Text © Tim Senior 2008
Editor and commissioning editor
Martin Derry
Colour profiles © Rolando Ugalini

The right of Tim Senior to be identified as
the author of this work has been asserted
in accordance with sections 77 and 78 of
the Copyright Designs and Patents Act,
1988.

Printed in England by
Ian Allan Printing Limited
Riverdene Business Park
Molesey Road
Hersham, Surrey
KT12 4RG
United Kingdom

Half title page: *Hastings T.5 TG505,
seen on finals at RAF Coningsby on
18th December 1972, either
experiencing engine trouble or
practising a three-engined
approach.* Terry Senior

Title page: *An early view of a
Hastings C.1 dropping supplies.
Smaller items were carried inside
the external canisters attached to
the underside of the forward
fuselage, whilst larger loads were
dispatched via the freight doors.*
Aeroplane via Handley Page
Association

Opposite page: *Photographed from
the side door of another Hastings.
Hastings C.1A TG527 bears the City
of Bath Coat of Arms on the fin.*
David Willis/ARC

CONTENTS

ACKNOWLEDGEMENTS
I would like to thank the following individuals for
their help and contributions with information and
photographs for this book.
Staff at the RAF Museum, Department of
Research and Information Services,
Adrian Balch, Denis Calvert, Martin Derry,
Harry Fraser-Mitchell/Handley Page Association,
Peter Green, Paul Jackson, Mike Smith curator
of the Newark Air Museum, Ray Sturtivant,
Steve Thompson, David Tuplin, Richard L Ward,
Brandon White, David Willis/ARC,
Jim Winchester, Matthew O'Sullivan Keeper
of Photographs RNZAF Museum,
Bernd von Kostka, Alliierten (Allied) Museum
Berlin, John Cooper and finally, my father
Terry Senior.
    The publishers would like to thank
Andy Thomas, Chris Salter, Neil Robinson,
Paul Lucas, Tony O'Toole, Brian Lowe and
Dave Sargent.

Chapter 1: **LOOKING TOWARDS THE FUTURE**

Towards the end of the Second World War, most British aircraft manufacturers began to look to the future peacetime needs of the Royal Air Force and the possibilities of post-war exports. Many interesting new designs emerged, some of which were quickly rendered outdated, due largely to new technology; i.e. the jet engine and improvements in construction and aerodynamics. It is perhaps surprising therefore to realise that some manufacturers continued to adapt and design new aircraft derived from existing older types. The need for a large dedicated fleet of long range transport aircraft, while important, was deemed not to be a great priority during Second World War, the emphasis being on mass production of fighter and bomber aircraft. RAF Transport Command had to rely solely on a combination of converted British types, or Lend-Lease aircraft from the United States.

Interim types

By the end of the war the RAF's transport fleet consisted of a number of aircraft types including the Douglas C-47 Dakota and various obsolete or obsolecent converted ex-bombers. Most of these had either been removed from bombing duties because they were simply too old, too slow or could not fly at sufficient altitude to avoid German anti-aircraft artillery. Those used in the transport role towards the end of the war included the Handley Page Harrow and Halifax, Short Stirling and Vickers Warwick. The order of battle for RAF Trans-

port Command in mid-1945 reveals several older types still in use, albeit principally for training purposes, including the Vickers Wellington, Armstrong-Whitworth Albemarle and Whitley. Some of those mentioned were used for glider-towing duties. Indeed the airborne forces perceived use of gliders was not totally abandoned at the cessation of hostilities. Gliders in use at this time included the Airspeed Horsa and the General Aircraft Ltd (GAL) Hamilcar. It was not total gloom however, as by July 1945 there were two RAF units operating the relatively recent Avro York. The York, adapted in part from the Avro Lancaster, incorporated a purpose-built freight capability.

Old Rivals

The principal manufacturers of the two most widely used heavy bombers for the RAF during the war, Avro and Handley Page (HP), were both heavily committed to production of the Lancaster and Halifax, with newer variants featuring various design changes and more powerful engines. Despite his workload, Sir Fredrick Handley Page had already identified a need for a post-war transport aircraft. In May 1942 he wrote to his chief designer G R Volkert proposing an aircraft based on the Halifax, but with a pressurised circular-section hull of at least 9ft in diameter with a parallel portion at least 12ft long. This was envisaged as being a freighter, troop transport and aerial tanker. It was also planned to be a bomber; un-pressurised for short

The Handley Page Halifax series of bombers led toward the development of the Hastings and Hermes family of aircraft. The first operational version of the Halifax was the HP57 B.I series I. This view illustrates a Halifax from the first production batch of 50 aircraft; L9530 was serving with 76 Squadron, from No 4 Group Bomber Command, based at Middleton St George, (known today as Durham Tees Valley airport). This aircraft crashed near Bremen, whilst returning from a raid on Berlin on the night of 12/13th August 1941. Pilot Officer Christopher Cheshire and four members of the aircrew became prisoners of war, while sadly two gunners were killed.
Handley Page Association

range and pressurised for long-range missions. Unfortunately the proposal was rejected when it was submitted to the Air Ministry as they had already given the go-ahead for the Avro York, which proved to be successful, the prototype having completed its first flight in July 1942. Undeterred by this rejection, HP submitted another design with the company designation HP64 in January 1943, which proposed a civil transport, essentially a Halifax with a new 9ft-diameter fuselage and retaining the familiar twin fins. Subsequent wind tunnel testing concluded that the fuselage diameter could be increased to 11ft with little penalty. The Air Ministry opposed the proposal as they were already studying the post war use of bomber aircraft, and because the York was already in production. The study, considering the use of bombers for post-war trooping and freight duties had been split into two potential categories: Transport A, which consisted of a stripped out airframe, with its armament retained, or, Transport B which was the same without armament. Several versions of Halifax were eventually selected and built, while others were converted to satisfy both of these proposed versions.

A proposal designated HP66 for a long range (Far East) bomber, developed from the Halifax, was made in mid-1943. By utilising the 113ft wing section from the HP66 for the proposed HP64 transport, Handley Page's director of technical development suggested (in April 1944) combining the wing with a new centre section, together with a new single fin. The combination of the two proposals, was designated HP67, and this was tendered to the Ministry of Aircraft Production. The proposal was approved.

Specification C3/44 had been issued by the Air Ministry in April 1944, calling for a multi-purpose transport to replace Halifax C.VIII freighter/passenger transporters and Halifax A.IX airborne forces transport

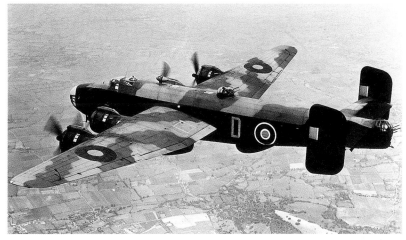

and glider tug. This effectively matched the HP67 and two prototype HP67s were ordered; and allocated serials TE580 and TE583. Handley Page were also keen to venture into the civil airline market, and gave priority to a civil version of the HP67 which became the pressurised HP68: the two designs were otherwise almost identical. The prototype HP68 however would be built without pressurisation, as it would simply serve only as a trials airframe. Handley Page had already chosen the Bristol Hercules radial engine as a powerplant for the new aircraft, having amassed a great deal of experience with this series of engine. They were unimpressed with the Rolls Royce Merlin as fitted to 2,965 early Halifax marks I and II, and switched to the Hercules instead, using it to power 3,212 later production Halifaxes. The only visible external difference between the engines used on the Halifax and those of the HP67 would be the use of streamlined low-drag engine nacelles. Early tests of the engines and nacelles destined for the HP67 were conducted on Halifax B.VI, RG642.

Top: *Merlin-engined Halifax B.V series IA LL219 in 1944. The unusual nose art is noteworthy as is that of the Halifax beyond.*
Brian Lowe

Above: *Eventually Handley Page were able to secure the use of Bristol Hercules engines in lieu of the Merlin, and the Halifax was transformed. HP had never been totally satisfied with the Merlin.*
Handley Page Association

A Civil version

Initially Handley Page gave more priority to the development of the civilian version, the HP68, later known as the Hermes I. In early 1945, there was significant indecision on the future of the Hermes, principally due to Avro having gained an advantage with the development of their Tudor airliner. This was not helped by the prevarication of the Ministry of Aircraft Production as to which aircraft it preferred, and who would receive a

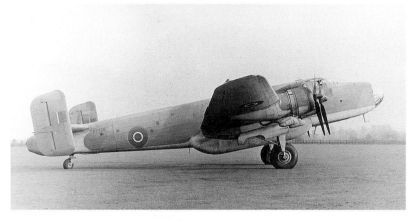

After the HP64 had been cancelled, Handley Page produced the Halifax C.VIII, initially referred to as Transport B, i.e. without armament. A large number of surplus RAF Halifax C.VIIIs were subsequently converted for use by civilian companies, including PP326 seen here and which later served with BOAC as G-AIAR.
Handley Page Association

production contract for the only potential customer, British Overseas Airways Corporation (BOAC). At the time, BOAC was the nationalised airline and independent airline companies did not exist. Most of the new carriers began forming only after the end of hostilities, and most did not appear until the end of 1945.

Construction work on the first prototype Hermes I began at Radlett in mid-1945, and was finally completed in November. The aircraft was allocated the civilian registration G-AGSS, while a second airframe was allocated G-AGUB. Although the first aircraft was little more than an empty shell, the second was duly completed as a fully equipped pressurised airframe. With ground taxi test runs completed on 1st December, the flight test took place at Handley Page's flight test airfield at Radlett, Hertfordshire. Sadly, an intended fast taxiing run on 2nd December ended in tragedy, when the aircraft left the ground inadvertently and uncontrollably after which the aircraft was seen to be suffering from extreme longitudinal instability, and after a few miles it climbed steeply, stalled and crashed inverted. The company test pilot Flt Lt James Talbot and his test observer E A 'Ginger' Wright were killed instantly. Despite the tragedy being a huge setback, work continued on both the HP67 and the Hermes after the accident. The investigation found that the cause was attributed to an overbalanced elevator, owing partly to an under-estimation of tab power. This lead to a misinterpretation of instructions, which in turn resulted in too high a tab gearing being set.

Construction and ground testing of the HP67, TE580 continued after a brief pause for the Hermes accident investigation, which was concluded during late January 1946. As a result of the accident to the first Hermes, the first HP67 prototype TE580 was dis-

mantled and moved by road to RAF Wittering, near Stamford in Lincolnshire; it being considered that the runway at Radlett was marginal in wet conditions. After it had been reassembled and undergone ground running tests, TE580 was deemed ready for its first flight. Handley Page had still to find a replacement test pilot, so Sqn Ldr Maurice Hartford was loaned to the company from the RAF to undertake initial trials. Sqn Ldr Hartford finally took TE580 into the air on 7th May 1946, performing a flight lasting 35 minutes, the aircraft cruising at a speed of 200mph and climbing to a height of 11,000ft; Hartford also performed numerous general handling manoeuvres. With testing continuing, the first aircraft was flown back to Radlett on 23rd May and was christened Hastings by the Mayor of Hastings, on 4th September. The town of Hastings is permanently etched into the history books, after the famous Battle of Hastings in October 1066, when King Harold was famously fatally wounded, during the invasion by William I. Many years later 1066 was used unofficially as a 'Squadron number' for the unit operating the last remaining Hastings in service. The first aircraft was joined in the test programme at the end of 1946 by the second prototype, TE583, which made its first flight from Radlett with Sqn Ldr Hartford at the controls on 30th December.

Service Trials

TE580 flew to Boscombe Down, Wiltshire, to commence Service Trials Acceptance with the Aeroplane and Armament Experimental Establishment (A&AEE). It was joined there by TE583 on 17th January 1947. Production of the first 100 Hastings C.1s had already commenced with the components being assembled at Cricklewood, north west London. The final assembly of major airframe components took place after a road journey to Radlett, where the first production Hastings TG499 made its maiden flight on 25th April 1947 in the hands of the newly appointed company test pilot, Sqn Ldr Hedley 'George' Hazelden. The flight, while successful, did however encounter rudder-tab flutter. Although subsequently fixed by 'cording' the trailing edge , this indicated all was not well with the aircraft's handling, indeed handling in some regions of the flight envelope were deemed unacceptable by test pilots at the A&AEE. As higher weights and more extended centre of gravity positions were investigated, the elevators were assessed to be heavy, and there was a degree of longitudinal instability when the aircraft was in the climb. This demanded constant attention from the pilot to prevent the nose rising, together with large changes of trim when operating the flaps. Initial changes by HP consisted of canting the engine thrustlines upwards by 2½ degrees, which didn't appear to make any improvement. TE580 went through progressive modifications to attempt to improve the problem, these included setting the tailplane to both 5 and 10-degree dihedral, together with 5, 10 and 15 degrees of anhedral. These trials were so important

Above: *Although most civilian Halifax VIIIs were used as freighters, some were converted to serve with BOAC as passenger aircraft and these were renamed Halton. One of the aircraft converted was G-AHDU which received the name Falkirk; it later served with Aviation Traders and Bond Air Services.* Handley Page Association

Below: *The Halifax A.IX (later A.9) was the definitive version used to support the airborne forces. RT760 the aircraft seen here, was the third production airframe built. Among the units that operated this version were No.47 and 297 Squadrons at Fairford.* Handley Page Association

Opposite top: *Hermes I prototype G-AGSS on 2nd December 1945, shortly before the aircraft crashed. At this stage there were few external differences between the Hermes and the Hastings.*
Handley Page Association

Opposite bottom: *TE580 captured moments into its first flight on 7th May 1946. Of note is the familiar yellow ringed 'P' denoting its prototype status.*
Handley Page Association.

that two production airframes, TG501 and TG502, were used for these trials over many years. Both underwent several tailplane alterations before it was concluded that moving the tailplane down 16 inches, and increasing the overall area of the tailplane would eventually solve the stability problems. The lowering of the tailplane was later adopted and incorporated into the design of the later C.2, C.3 and C.4 variants. It was not fitted retrospectively to surviving C.1s, or its derivatives the C.1A, MET.1 and T.5.

Early production aircraft were also involved in glider-towing trials when, on 1st April 1947, TG501 became the first Hastings to fly with a GAL Hamilcar in tow. The trials continued when TG501 transferred to the Airborne Forces Experimental Establishment, at Beaulieu, Hampshire on 16th August. Meanwhile TG499 undertook para drops from 5th February 1948 and TG500 had carrier beams installed to permit heavy external loads to be dropped by parachute. As part of the test programme, Handley Page used TG503 to undertake an extended overseas flight test and route proving exercise. The aircraft effectively embarked on an overseas mini-tour when on 11th March 1948 it departed from RAF Lyneham, Wiltshire, heading for Australia and New Zealand. After departing Lyneham the aircraft was routed via Malta, Habbaniya in Iraq then onto Pakistan and India, stopping at Negombo in Ceylon, (now Sri Lanka), before flying

its final leg from Singapore to Darwin then onwards to Sydney after a total of 46½ hours in the air. This was the first time that a new British type had performed such a long distance flight before entering service. The aircraft then departed to its final outbound destination, New Zealand. The tour lasted for a total of four months and the aircraft carried a mixed crew of RAF and HP personnel together with observers from the Ministry of Supply (MoS). The aircraft performed perfectly, apart from one engine failure on the flight from Sydney to Brisbane caused by an oil pump failure. Despite this a great deal of valuable information covering operations away from a home base was obtained. This included the performance of the aircraft while operating in tropical conditions and into small airfields such as Paraparaumu in New Zealand.

Meanwhile back in Britain, trials continued apace and the need to start deliveries to the RAF increased, and as a result on 1st June 1948, the Hastings received its Controller (Aircraft) release to service.

The first prototype Hastings seen running its engines at RAF Wittering in May 1946, shortly before its first test flight. An unidentified Halifax stands in the foreground. The Halifax continued in RAF squadron service until 1952, although the last Halifax in RAF service was an A.9 which survived until retired in August 1954.
Handley Page Association.

Above: *During its first flight TE580 was taken up to an altitude of 11,000 feet and achieved a cruising speed of 200 mph. It was airborne for a total of 35 minutes.*
Handley Page Association.

Right: *A head on view of TE580 during one of its early test flights in 1946. Note the low drag engine nacelles and the intakes for the oil cooler and air injection intakes.*
Handley Page Association.

Right: *Still wearing its prototype identification markings, Hastings prototype TE580 seen at Stansted in June 1962.*
Tony Eastwood collection

Above: *The second Hastings prototype, TE583 later served as an engine test bed and is seen here in 1949, with a pair of Armstrong Siddeley Sapphire engines fitted into outboard engine pods. The aircraft also served as a trials airframe for a HP Victor escape door.* David Willis/ARC

Below: *Photographs of the second prototype are seemingly limited to the period when TE583 served as an engine test bed for the Sapphire engine.* Handley Page Association

Opposite top: *Handley Page workers carefully align the fuselage to the wing centre section of a Hastings during final assembly at Radlett.* Handley Page Association

Opposite bottom: *A view of the final assembly line at Radlett, with a quantity of mostly complete Hastings C.1s visible. The centre section mainplane for another is visible in the foreground.* Handley Page Association

Above: *Viewed from the other end of the final assembly hall, these Hastings C.1s already have roundels and fin flashes, and blue cheat-line applied. All remain unidentifiable, with the exception of the second airframe in the middle row, partially identified as TG51..* Handley Page Association

Below: *TE580 is seen here in a posed publicity shot, shortly after its naming ceremony in 1946, together with some of its intended users in the foreground.* Handley Page Association

Right and below: Two photographs illustrating the different experimental configurations trialled on TE580. In an attempt to cure the longitudinal instability problems the top photograph shows the dihedral tailplane, while the centre illustration shows the widened anhedral version.
Handley Page Association and Ray Sturtivant

Right: *The fourth production Hastings C.1, TG502, seen here fitted with the successful experimental lowered tailplane.* Ray Sturtivant

Left and below: *The loading ramp for the Hastings is seen being manoeuvred towards TG523. Once the ramps were attached to it small vehicles such as this jeep could be driven aboard.* Both Handley Page Association

Bottom: *This photograph illustrates the roller track, which was occasionally fitted inside the fuselage of the Hastings.* Handley Page Association

Chapter 2: **COLD WAR AND WEATHER**

Hastings deliveries to the first RAF squadron commenced during September 1948, when No.47 Squadron, having relinquished its Halifax A.9s at RAF Fairford, Gloucestershire, moved to RAF Dishforth in North Yorkshire. The unit received its first aircraft direct from Radlett towards the end of the month. By late October they had received another twelve Hastings, nine from the manufacturer and three from temporary storage at 5 Maintenance Unit (MU), at RAF Kemble, Gloucestershire, these included TG510, TG514, TG517, TG519 and TG530. The aircrew conversion process went well, although it wasn't completely without incident, as the unit suffered the first loss of a Hastings on 2nd October. While performing a three-engine approach aboard TG519, the crew undershot the runway in turbulent conditions. The Hastings' port wing struck trees, following which the aircraft hit the runway and the port undercarriage was torn off. Despite this, the airframe was essentially intact and, though deemed to be a write-off, it subsequently became a ground instructional airframe. At this point normal RAF peacetime work-up procedures for a new aircraft were effectively abandoned as the Hastings was about to be thrust into the Berlin Airlift.

Berlin

Following the end of the Second World War, the victorious nations of Great Britain, France, United States and USSR, maintained occupying forces within Germany which was split into two, East and West Germany. The Soviet Union maintained occupying forces in the East, whilst the other nations occupied the West. The German capital Berlin lay inside Soviet occupied Germany and as the hostilities concluded, the three Western Powers created respective occupation zones in the Western sector of Berlin, leaving the Russians maintaining a single zone in the remainder. Unfortunately it was a very uneasy peace, with the Soviets generally opposed to almost everything the Western powers did. The Allies access to Berlin consisted of three rail and three road routes into the city. All traffic entering Berlin was monitored by the Russians and on the 31st March 1948 they announced all road traffic would be inspected. Following an incident when a US military train was stopped the following day, the US Air Force commenced operations to fly all supplies into the city. In early June the three nations in the Western sector of Berlin, made the decision to formally create a single West German state. Naturally the Soviets were bitterly opposed to this, realising that it would undermine the East German economy. All rail routes into the capital were stopped on 15th June, leaving the British no alternative but to re-supply its garrisons by air. The situation escalated further on the 24th when all road traffic into the capital was cut. The Soviets issued a statement stating that it would not supply food for the 2.25 million Berliners living in the western sector.

An early formation of three RAF Hastings C.1s, illustrating the original High Speed Silver colour scheme, with blue cheat-line.
Handley Page Association

Please refer to the explanatory note 'The Colour Silver' regarding High Speed Silver on page 76.

Above: *Other than the cheat-line early production Hastings left the factory unpainted, as illustrated in this air-to-air view of the 10th production airframe, TG508. It is possible that these early Hastings were rushed into service unpainted because they were urgently required to participate in the Berlin Airlift.* Newark Air Museum Collection

Below: *German labourers take a short break at Schleswigland while preparing an area for a new hardstanding to be laid; the Hastings at the front is TG530. Of interest in the background are the Airspeed Horsa gliders, which were still in use by Transport Command for training in 1948.* Handley Page Association.

The Berlin Airlift, *Operation Plainfare,* commenced on 26th June 1948. RAF Transport Command aircraft that participated included Dakotas, Halifaxes and Yorks, joined by numerous civilian airline and airfreight companies. The latter operated a variety of aircraft including Halifaxes and Haltons, Avro Lancastrians, Tudors and Yorks. Several operators also used Bristol Freighters, while one operated Vickers Vikings, and many others operated the Dakota. Despite this multitude of aircraft, there was an urgent need for more to maintain the airlift. One of the main RAF airfields in use by Transport Command at the time was Schleswigland in northern Germany, close to the border with Denmark. A request for assistance was received and No.47 Squadron quickly deployed there, dispatching a total of eight aircraft on 1st November. The first sortie flown by 47 Squadron commenced from Schleswigland on 11th November with the journey of 400 miles taking 2½ hours.

In Britain the delivery of aircraft and the conversion process was well underway with the delivery of TG531 to Dishforth on the 5th November. The second squadron chosen to convert to the Hastings was No. 297 Squadron, which had also operated Halifax A.9s alongside No.47 at Fairford. It too moved to Dishforth on 17th October 1948, and following aircrew training departed to Schleswigland at the end of November, thus boosting the RAF's heavy-lift presence on Airlift duties. The cargo carried on these flights was mainly coal especially over the winter months, however flour and other materials were carried. The Hastings was one of only a few types available to carry girders and the associated cooling tubes for use in the construction of a power station in West Berlin. Some of the girders measured 1½ feet wide, 4 feet deep and 32 feet long, and weighed almost 7,000lbs. Petrol was also carried by the Hastings, after shortages began to tell in January 1949, eighteen flights were hurriedly arranged with each aircraft carrying twenty 40-gallon drums. Not surprisingly with the high tempo of operations during the Berlin Airlift, there were minor accidents, including TG510, which was forced to make a crash landing after having sunk down on to its already retracting undercarriage on take-off. Although this rendered the undercarriage extension and retraction mechanism practically useless, the aircraft was recovered and repaired. Failure of the tail wheel self centering device also created a few incidents; the cause was suspected to have been groundcrew failing to use the locking device when towing aircraft on the ground. In a separate incident, Hastings TG611 crashed on take-off from Tegel airfield on 16th July 1949, with the nose-up trim still set, the resultant steep climb-out caused it to stall from which the aircraft failed to recover and all five aircrew were killed.

The blockade of Berlin officially ended on 12th May 1949, although a third squadron, No.53, had converted to the Hastings from Dakotas on 1st August and continued to participate during the winding up phase

of *Operation Plainfare*. No.47 Squadron returned to RAF Topcliffe, near Dishforth on 22nd August together with elements of 53 Squadron. The last Hastings flight of the Airlift occurred on 6th September. No.297 Squadron and the remaining crews from 53 moved to Wunsdorf in West Germany, returning to Topcliffe on 13th December.

During the operation a total of 32 Hastings had taken part, moving 55,000 tons of cargo, in 12,396 sorties totalling 16,385 flying hours, an *average* lift of 4.4 tons of cargo per flight. The Airlift in total conveyed 2¼ million tons of material, two-thirds of which was coal to West Berlin.

Return to normal operations

Hastings trials had continued in Britain with, amongst others TG512 which was assigned to the Transport Command Development Flight. This aircraft took part in container dropping trials at Beaulieu, which commenced on 27th January 1949. Before the end of the month, the aircraft had successfully proved that it could drop twenty-four 350lb containers in 4½ seconds. The Hastings was intended to be capable of carrying a wide variety of loads internally; several trials had included a Jeep with either a trailer or a six-pound anti-tank gun. Other loads would include 30 paratroopers and 20 supply containers, whilst in the casualty evacuation role it could be fitted with 32 stretchers, with room for 28 sitting wounded, four medical attendants and medical supplies, or, up to 50 passengers in rear facing seats. There was an intention to use an air-dropped container known as the Universal Freight Container or the Paratechnicon. This extremely bulky device was about 35 feet long and approximately 10ft^2 and was capable of carrying loads of up to 13,500lbs. These trials were conducted using the first production Hastings, TG499, which made its first flight from Hatfield, Hertfordshire with the device attached on 13th May 1949. This did however reduce the top speed of the aircraft by 24 knots. TG499 performed trials at Farnborough with the RAE, it then moved to the A&AEE at Boscombe Down on the 14th September. On its second flight on 26th September, the pannier broke free at the front as the aircraft was returning to base, it swung backwards and sliced off the starboard tailplane. After a series of climbing and diving turns, the aircraft crashed at Beacon Hill near Amesbury, Wiltshire, sadly all three aircrew were killed.

At RAF Dishforth, Hastings deliveries continued enabling No.241 Operational Conversion Unit (OCU) to re-equip from January 1950 and commence aircrew training on the Hastings. After the end of operations in Berlin the squadrons were able to return to their more regular duties including long-range route flying, and supporting the airborne forces, amongst others.

At RAF Lyneham in Wiltshire, a second wing of Hastings was in the process of forming from August

1949 onwards. Nos.99 and 511 Squadrons relinquished their Yorks to re-equip with the Hastings in August and September respectively. There was however another Hastings squadron which also re-equipped at Lyneham in August 1949. No.242 Squadron is almost always overlooked in any reference to the Hastings history, however, from August 1949 to 1st May 1950 the Squadron was equipped with the Hastings. Its first Commanding Officer was Sqn Ldr N M Maynard DFC AFC (later Air Marshal Sir Nigel Maynard). The Squadron was employed principally in flying the strategic trunk routes to the Far East. Its existance with the Hastings was short-lived and No.242 disbanded on 1st May 1950. Perhaps the existence of No.242 Squadron and No.242 OCU (formed in 1951) may have created confusion! The next unit to begin conversion to the Hastings was No.24 Squadron at Lyneham in December 1950, although a portion of its aircrew were transferred from No.297 Squadron which had disbanded at Topcliffe on 15th November 1950. As a result of the disbandment the Topcliffe wing was short by one squadron, therefore No.24 Squadron was transferred to Topcliffe in January 1951 to compensate. A subsequent reorganisation of the Hastings units required No.53 Squadron to join Nos.99 and 511 at Lyneham on 9th February. This enabled the Lyneham Hastings to concentrate on performing long distance supply operations, mainly to the Far East, with flights staging to Changi in Singapore. They also performed supply flights to bases in both Cyprus and the Middle East. As a direct result of the Korean War which commenced in June 1950, aircraft flying to Singapore had also to include Japan to its list of destinations. Meanwhile both No.24 and No.47 Squadrons remained at Topcliffe and performed the more specialised role of supporting the airborne forces. No.241 OCU remained at Dishforth performing the aircrew conversion role, before eventually incorporating the additional role of medium transport conversion from No.240 OCU based at North Luffenham, Rutland. Ultimately Nos.240 and 241 OCUs merged to form No.242 OCU on 16th April 1951.

Hastings for Coastal Command

The next unit to commence conversion to the Hastings performed an entirely different role altogether. No.202 Squadron operated Halifaxes in the early post war years within RAF Coastal Command, performing Meteorological flights over the North Atlantic. Two contracts were originally issued to convert Hastings C.1s into MET.1s, although the first order for thirteen was reduced to the following aircraft: TG565, TG566, TG567, TG576, TG616, TG620, TG621, TG622, TG623, and TG624. A second batch originally for fourteen further conversions was subsequently cut to eight and comprised the following: TG504, TG505, TG507, TG510, TG511, TG514, TG516, and TG517. The unit never operated all these conversions, as many were placed into storage and never flew a single MET sortie, indeed several were eventually converted back to C.1s. The conversion process entailed fitting the aircraft with a meteorological observers position in place of the second pilot, as well as fitting the aircraft with various sensors, bunks and a galley. The MET.1s were also fitted with Lindholme dinghy containers for air sea

Work carried on in almost any weather during the Berlin Airlift. Groundcrews are seen with TG527 on a bitter winter's day.
Handley Page Association

rescue purposes. The first such conversion to fly was TG620 on 27th September 1950 and was the first Hastings delivered to No.202 Squadron at Aldergrove, Northern Ireland on 2nd November. The unit flew missions west bound in a triangular pattern, under the codename *Bismuth* passing weather data obtained back to base each hour for onward relay to the Central Forecasting Office in the UK.

Hastings production and modification

Production of the Hastings C.1 (including MET.1 conversions) continued until the delivery of the 100th C.1 TG624, which made its first flight on 8th February 1950. With C.1 production complete, Handley Page switched to production of the improved C.2, which incorporated the larger lower mounted tailplane as trialled on C.1 TG502. Other improvements incorporated into the C.2 included three flexible fuel tanks added to both outer wings. The first C.2, WD475, made its first flight on 14th November 1950, and was the first of 65 C.2s ordered. However, this quantity was subsequently reduced to just 25, serialled WD475 to WD499. Deliveries of C.2s commenced in March 1951, when both WD477 and WD478 were handed over to the RAF's handling squadron to enable the pilot's notes to be written. Having entered service the increased range of the C.2 proved so useful that a programme to upgrade the C.1 was also conducted. A decision was taken to convert approximately 50 surviving C.1s to as near C.2 standard as possible; they were redesignated C.1A, commencing with TG501. Their tailplanes were not modified, however fuel capacity was increased by the adoption of external underwing fuel tanks, (not drop-tanks despite their appearance). Internally the C.1A received an updated Mark 9 auto-pilot and winterised oil tanks in addition to other minor upgrades.

Despite reducing the first production batch of C.2s from 65 to 25 aircraft (WD475 to WD499) a 26th airframe was retained to emerge eventually as the first Hastings C.4, with the serial WD500. This version was intended to serve purely as a VIP aircraft and three further C.4s were ordered, these being included in a batch of 20 Hastings, the remaining 17 of which were built as C.2s. The C.4s received serials WJ324 to WJ326 and the 17 C.2s were serialled WJ327 to WJ343.

WD500 made its first flight on 22nd September 1951, and differed from standard freight aircraft in that it featured a set of hydraulically operated folding stairs, which were attached to the main passenger door. The transport freight doors were deleted on the C.4s leaving just the passenger door that opened out and downwards, as opposed to being side hinged. Apart from two extra windows on the port side, these were the only major external differences between the C.4 and C.2 Hastings. Commencing early in 1953, most of the RAF Hastings fleet was refitted with more reliable and powerful Hercules engines, replacing the earlier Hercules 101, as fitted to all C.1s and Hercules 106 fitted to early production C.2s. Hastings C.1As were re-engined during their modification programme from C.1s.

Trials and exports

As well as serving the RAF, the Hastings served with various government experimental and research organisations in the United Kingdom. Due to its large size, it made an ideal trials and test aircraft. One of the first Hastings selected for dedicated trials was the sixth C.2, WD480, which was flown from Aston Down, Gloucestershire to Radlett on 3rd July 1951. The aircraft was fitted with a long pannier on the underside of the fuselage. One of WD480s first tasks was concerned with sonobuoy trials, the pannier being equipped with three sets of doors for stowage of various types of sonobuoy. The fuselage was divided into two, with a laboratory at the front and an area at the rear for a launching tube and racks for marker buoys and ample room for technicians. With the conversion finished the aircraft was delivered to the Royal Aircraft Establishment (RAE) at Farnborough, Hampshire on 1st April 1953. The RAE operated a number of Hastings until the early/mid-1970s.

The second prototype, TE583, was returned to Handley Page and following modification, emerged with a pair of Armstrong Siddeley Sapphire jet engines, that would ultimately power the Handley Page Victor fitted into the outboard engine pods. During its trials for the forthcoming Victor, TE583 was fitted with a trial Victor escape door and displayed two leading edge profile markings on the rear fuselage as part of the experiments with the door. The aircraft was passed onto the Royal Radar Establishment in 1954 and took part in numerous radar trials programmes.

Another test establishment that used Hastings for trials and transport work was the A&AEE at Boscombe Down. Amongst the various aircraft used were the second and fourth production Hastings TG500 and TG502.

The first and only export order for the Hastings was placed by the Royal New Zealand Air Force (RNZAF). The earlier visit to New Zealand by TG503 was instrumental in gaining the order for just four Hastings. These were designated Hastings C.3 and were based on the RAF's C.2. However, the C.3 incorporated uprated Hercules 737 engines, which gave a better performance albeit at the expense of cruising economy at high altitude. The RNZAF Hastings incorporated extensive instrument and radio changes in comparison with the C.2s and received the company designation HP95 as a result of all these changes. The first C.3 NZ5801 flew on 2nd November 1952. After their delivery flights to New Zealand all four aircraft were initially operated by the Hastings Flight of No.41 Squadron, until the unit was re-numbered No.40 in December 1954. NZ5804 was the last new build Hastings to be completed.

A view of the flightline at Schleswigland, taken from the freight door of another Hastings. The two nearest identifiable aircraft are TG524 and TG526. Handley Page Association

A close-up view of the loading process onto TG526. This photograph illustrates to advantage the parachute door included within the freight door. Handley Page Association

Handley Page developed a loading ramp to assist with awkward outsized cargo. Handley Page Association

Above: *Two views of various cargo loads aboard a Hastings during the Berlin Airlift. The view above right shows water-cooling pipes destined for the West Berlin power station.* Handley Page Association

Right: *The Berlin Airlift was not without incident. This photograph illustrates the burnt-out front fuselage of Hastings TG534 at Schleswigland on 6th April 1949. The incident was caused by failure to lock the fuel drain cock, and the resulting fire occurred during start up. While both the engines and the wings remained relatively unscathed, the cockpit and fuselage have almost completely disintegrated.* Handley Page Association

Below: *Access to the Hastings was gained via the freight door at the rear, a door underneath the rear fuselage, or via the rather steeper boarding ladder method illustrated here. The ladder could be folded and stowed away within the Air Quartermaster's station.* Handley Page Association

Right: *External supply canisters seen here shortly after release from C.1 TG568.*
Handley Page Association

Below: *The Hastings supported the British Army during deployments and exercises abroad. The RAF and RNZAF Hastings could also be fitted for casualty evacuation if required.*
David Willis/ARC

Opposite page: *Two views of early production Hastings C.2s in the early overall High Speed Silver colour scheme. Top, WD479 served solely as a transport aircraft with the RAF. Bottom, WD480 was eventually used as a trials airframe with the Royal Aircraft Establishment at Farnborough.*
Both David Willis/ARC

Opposite page top: *As well as carrying cargo both internally and externally, the Hastings also carried paratroops in the airborne support role. Several paratroops are seen here making their exit through both port and starboard passenger doors.* David Willis/ARC

Opposite page bottom: *Hastings C.4 WJ326 at Northolt in December 1964 carrying RAF Middle East titles. The main external difference between the VIP C.4 and transport versions was the deletion of the freight door and the addition of folding stairs. While the air stairs are not visible in this photograph, the hinges for the downward opening passenger door clearly are.* Tony Eastwood

Top: *Hastings C.4, WD500 illustrates the wider cheat-line applied to this version. The undersides are highly polished.* David Willis/ARC

Above: *All RAF Transport Command aircraft were fitted with rearward facing seats, as illustrated in this view looking forward inside a Hastings.* Handley Page Association

Right: *The folding air-stairs on the VIP Hastings C.4 were attached to the door of the aircraft.* Handley Page Association

Top: *The Hastings MET.1s of Coastal Command were originally painted in Medium Sea Grey upper surfaces with white undersides as illustrated on TG616, seen here on a pre-delivery test flight.* Handley Page Association

Above: *The first major colour scheme change for the RAF Hastings fleet occurred towards the end of 1951. The addition of white fuselage upper surfaces is illustrated on C.1 TG554 of No.242 OCU during March 1952.* Brandon White

Top: *Hastings from Coastal and Transport Commands at the RAF Coronation Review, RAF Odiham, in July 1953. Hastings C.1 TG560 is in the early colour scheme devoid of any squadron markings.* Newark Air Museum

Above: *Hastings MET.1 TG622 at RAF Odiham. It is the subject of the colour 4-view on pages 94 and 95. via Brian Lowe*

Left: *Hastings C.2 WJ327, at the Coronation Review. This aircraft served with the RAF Flying College, Manby, Lincolnshire.* Newark Air Museum

Chapter 3: **HERMES DEVELOPMENT CONTINUES**

Undaunted by the crash of the Hermes prototype G-AGSS, Handley Page continued development using the second prototype G-AGUB. This aircraft would eventually undergo a far more radical change than was ever applied to the Hastings.

The first change proposed by Handley Page was to lengthen the fuselage; this involved inserting two new sections or 'plugs' into the front and rear of the existing fuselage. With these installed G-AGUB became the Hermes II with a length of 95 feet 6 inches as opposed to the original 82 feet 2 inch of the Mark I and acquired the company designation HP74. G-AGUB made a successful first flight on 2nd September 1947. Further changes were proposed with the inclusion of a tricycle undercarriage for the production version, later to become the Hermes IV, with company designation HP81. Handley Page proposed two versions: a 52-seat interior with seats set 4 abreast, or a 64-seat version with seating set 5 abreast. BOAC however, had its own thoughts as to the planned interior, and the manufacturer was told to supply the aircraft unfurnished.

Although the Hermes II was to have been equipped with Hercules 120 engines, in fact Hercules 130s were fitted. A proposal existed to use Bristol Theseus engines in a development of the Mark II, known as the HP79 Hermes III. The Mark III never left the drawing board, while the Hermes IV eventually emerged powered by four Hercules 763 engines. G-AGUB was transferred to the A&AEE at Boscombe Down on 9th July 1948, for comparative stability trials against a standard Hastings. This aircraft was also used as a test bed for the Hercules 763 engine, with two fitted in the outer wing positions, and undertook high temperature trials for these engines at both Idris in Libya, and Khartoum in Sudan during August 1949. With these trials successfully completed the aircraft returned to Radlett to regain a pair of Hercules 130s, completing further testing with Handley Page. The Aircraft was passed on to the Ministry of Supply test fleet in early 1952, acquiring the serial VX234 and it served with the Telecommunications Research Establishment (TRE) at Defford, which later became the Royal Radar Establishment and moved to Pershore, until it was finally retired in 1968.

The Hermes II never entered production. The Hermes IV, fitted with a tricycle undercarriage did enter into production following various delays concerning weight distribution and other design changes. Further delays were created by BOAC disagreeing over the internal layout, including the galley, amongst other things, although these problems were set aside. The first production aircraft G-AKFP made its first flight,

successfully, at Radlett on 5th September 1948. There were some teething troubles with the new undercarriage, including faulty forgings and steering problems with the nosewheel. Once these were sorted out the aircraft flew to Boscombe Down on 24th April 1949, for trials with the A&AEE. After one of the test flights, an inspection found a fatigue failure in the bulkhead under the tailplane; following modification, the aircraft returned to Radlett at the end of May. Production of the aircraft continued with all the airframes being registered to BOAC, the second production aircraft became G-ALDA, while the remaining aircraft ran in sequence through to G-ALDY with the exception of G-ALDQ.

Development of the Theseus powered Hermes V had also begun, with the first aircraft, G-ALEU, making its initial flight on 23rd August 1949 with Hedley Hazelden at the controls. While the aircraft was engaged in trials work, it suffered an engine fire and was forced to make a wheels-up landing at Chilbolton airfield, Hampshire on 10th April 1951; the aircraft was badly damaged and was deemed to be a write off. The aircraft was replaced with the second Hermes V, G-ALEV, which spent some time at both Boscombe Down and Farnborough performing trials until 1958. Aviation Traders later purchased the airframe and used the fuselage for freight door trials. Other proposed Hermes versions included a lighter version of the Mark IV, which was given the designation HP91 and would have become the Hermes VI. A final version, the Hermes VII was planned, and would have been fitted with Rolls Royce Griffon engines and was referred to as the HP92; neither the HP91 nor HP92 entered production.

Hermes in Service

The first deliveries of Hermes IVs to BOAC began in February 1950, almost a year later than planned due to delays from subcontractors and various airframe modifications. Seven aircraft were used for intensive crew training until August, although this did not go totally to plan as G-ALDF landed with its undercarriage retracted at Hurn, Dorset on 1st May. The incident was attributed to pilot error, the aircraft was repaired and re-entered service. BOAC introduced its Hermes onto routes between the UK and East and West Africa. The aircraft were initially painted silver overall, with the BOAC 'Speedbird' logo on the nose just below the cockpit. This colour scheme soon gave way to white upper fuselages, with a thick dark blue cheat-line and silver undersides; the aircraft that made the inaugural flight to West Africa on 6th August 1950 wore this scheme.

Opposite page:

Top: *This early view of the only Hermes II G-AGUB gives an idea of the difference between it and the Hermes I after the fuselage was lengthened.* Handley Page Association

Bottom: *The only Hermes II, G-AGUB spent its early trials days with Handley Page before being transferred to the TRE.* Handley Page Association

Opposite page:

Top: *Only two prototype Hermes Vs were built, the first of these being G-ALEU, which was written off during the flight test programme after a crash landing at Chilbolton.* Handley Page Association

Bottom: *An early photograph of the third production Hermes IV, G-ALDB, illustrating the silver scheme worn by BOAC aircraft. This aircraft was named* Hebe *and was destroyed in a crash at Pithiviers, France on 23rd July 1952 while on lease to Airwork, when it carried the trooping serial WZ839. This aircraft was travelling between the UK and Malta when the starboard outer engine disintegrated and damaged the inboard engine. Despite the crash all 77 people aboard survived. A little over one month later WZ841 (G-ALDF) was also lost off Sicily.* Newark Air Museum

The Hermes suffered from a number of incidents during its early service life, G-ALDH lost its propeller and reduction gear from the number four engine, the remains hitting the number three engine in the process. Despite this, the aircraft made a safe emergency landing at Lyon in France on 17th December 1951. G-ALDI lost its number three engine and its reduction gear entirely after a similar occurrence over Africa on 28th February 1952. The Hermes landed safely at Tripoli in Libya with a large gash in the side of the fuselage, which caused the first officer some minor injuries. On 26th May G-ALDN crash-landed in the Sahara desert after a navigational error, thankfully the tough construction of the Hermes saved the crew and passengers, although the First Officer later died from heat exhaustion before they were rescued. Despite several more accidents the Hermes was never grounded. Although the aircraft only had a relatively short career with BOAC, it was destined to remain active for quite a number of years with other companies.

Airwork Limited initially leased four aircraft for military trooping flights, these received rearward facing seats and some floor modifications. Other companies soon followed when BOAC retired the entire fleet during 1953; several independent airlines either leased or bought the surplus aircraft which were at that time still reasonably new airframes. These included Britavia, and Skyways, the latter starting a regular service between London and Singapore in 1955. Airwork soon found its acquisition rewarded with a 2½ year trooping flight contract, ferrying British Army troops to the Far East from 1954. Following the unfortunate loss of two DH Comets, BOAC were forced to reintro-

duce several Hermes into service, meanwhile both Britavia and Skyways quickly secured contracts ferrying troops to both the Middle and Far East. The Hermes operated by Airwork were painted with white tops and silver undersides and with a blue cheat-line down the length of the fuselage, together with 'AIRWORK LTD LONDON' titles along the top half of the fuselage. When engaged on trooping flights the company titles were removed, and replaced by military serial numbers, small RAF fin flashes and roundels for diplomatic reasons. Towards the end of the 1950s several of the ex-BOAC Hermes were operated by a few other airlines, including Falcon Airways, and Silver City in the UK, while a pair flew with Bahamas Airways and single examples with Middle East Airways and Air Safaris. All but one Hermes IV were sold for scrap after retirement, the exception being the Hemes IV fuselage which survives today within the Imperial War Museum at Duxford airfield, Cambridgeshire. Although it lost its wings while serving as a ground-based cabin trainer at Gatwick, G-ALDG underwent restoration in 2006 and, following a re-spray into BOAC colours, was installed inside the 'AIRSPACE' section of the museum.

Below: *The principal visual difference between the Hermes II and prototype Hermes IV, G-AKFP, was the installation of a tricycle undercarriage. It is seen at Radlett wearing the BOAC Speedbird logo.* Handley Page Association

Right: *G-ALDJ was named Hengist, and is seen in the later BOAC colour scheme.* Newark Air Museum

Centre: *Passengers walk to an unidentified Hermes IV, at Eastleigh airport Nairobi, Kenya.* Handley Page Association

Bottom: *The first production Hermes IV G-AKFP, was also used by Airwork Ltd, and was allocated the serial XD632 for trooping flights. Note the line up of Meteor night fighters in the background.* Newark Air Museum

Opposite top: *This aircraft appears to be G-ALDP, which had been named Homer when owned by BOAC. The aircraft went on to serve with the independent airline Britavia, the parent company of Silver City airlines where it gained the serial XJ269. It later served with Silver City by whom it was renamed City of Truro before being flown to Stansted for retirement and eventual scrapping on 10th October 1962.* Newark Air Museum

Opposite centre: *Silver City operated G-ALDG, the fuselage of which survives as an exhibit in the IWM Airspace exhibition at Duxford.* Handley Page Association

Opposite bottom: *Hermes IV G-ALDA is seen here during its service with Air Links, while visiting the Biggin Hill Air Fair. At the end of 1964 it was retired and flown to Southend, and subsequently broken up the following year.* Newark Air Museum

Above, right and below:
*Three views of Hermes
performing trooping flights
illustrate the policy of
carrying RAF style serials
and markings. The first
aircraft is unidentifiable
while the second and third
is WZ840 (G-ALDC), which
was named Hermione in
BOAC service. Initially
leased, and eventually
purchased by Airwork
Limited, the aircraft went
on to serve with Falcon
Airways, who renamed it
James Robertson Justice.
It crashed on landing at
Southend on 9th October
1960.*
All Newark Air Museum

Top: *Hermes IV G-ALDL is seen at Southend on 27th October 1962, wearing the colour scheme of Air Safaris, although it has had all the company titles removed.*

Centre: *G-ALDT with one engine removed and still wearing basic Skyways colours when seen at Southend on 27th October 1962.*

Above: *Silver City Hermes G-ALDU* City of Gloucester *also seen in storage at Southend on 27th October 1962. The sign propped against the nose wheel reads 'THIS AIRCRAFT IS NOT SCRAP KEEP OFF'. G-ALDU had earlier in its life been used for troop carrying for which it wore the so-called trooping serial XJ288.* All Newark Air Museum

Opposite page:

Top: *Another Hermes used by Silver City, G-ALDI is seen awaiting its fate at Southend in October 1962, ominously close to a pile of aircraft scrap. The Airline itself and its parent company Britavia, became part of British United Airways in 1962. This aircraft had received the serial XJ309 when used for trooping duties.* Newark Air Museum

Centre: *During its trials career the Hermes II prototype had a pannier fitted underneath the fuselage.* Adrian Balch Archive

Bottom: *After serving with Handley Page, Hermes II G-AGUB was passed onto the Telecommunications Research Establishment at Defford, Worcestershire. This later became the Royal Radar Establishment and moved to Pershore. Displaying its military serial VX234, this image was taken during a trials sortie in 1964.* Adrian Balch Archive

Top: *Another view of the only Hermes II, VX234 seen during take-off from Pershore, shortly before the aircraft was retired.*
Adrian Balch Archive

Above: *Another view of the sole surviving Hermes G-ALDG while it was serving with Silver City and named* City of Chester, *during a visit to RAF Manston, Kent, in February 1962.* Newark Air Museum

Chapter 4: 'WAR and PEACE' (AND REORGANISATION)

It has often been stated that since the last day of the Second World War until the present, British armed forces have been in conflict or potential conflict somewhere around the globe. Many of these may perhaps be regarded as mere skirmishes or bush fire wars, the inference being that they could be very minor incidents, although, for the forces concerned, just as deadly as any major conflict.

Whilst a few Hastings were removed for upgrading, repair or modification at any one time, the remainder undertook routine operations worldwide, not always conducted in response to, or threat of conflict. Routine tasks were the norm although they could of course be called upon to assist in other areas too. One such occasion occurred during the unprecedented flooding of the eastern low-lying counties of England during the disastrous floods there in May 1953. Hastings were used to fly sandbags to the affected areas in addition to other urgently required supplies.

Far from UK shores, Hastings were instrumental in supporting the British North Greenland Expedition which had been landed by RAF Short Sunderland flying boats on the Greenland coast in August 1952. The six members of the expedition then trekked to their principal camp site several hundred miles inland, at which location Hastings would drop supplies. Hastings WD492 of No.47 Squadron from RAF Topcliffe was detached to the USAF base, Thule, on the west coast of Greenland, from where it would supply the Expedition. The aircraft captain was F/Lt Mike Clancy.

The Hastings could be fitted with seating for a little more comfort. The seats were rear facing; standard RAF practice.
Newark Air Museum

Because WD492 was unable to land on the snow and in order to save on the cost of parachutes it was decided that certain stores would be thrown from the aircraft from an altitude of 50 feet. This decision had been influenced by French Air Force experience, when in support of one of their Arctic expeditions supplies had successfully been dropped from 10 metres (33 feet). This altitude was too low for the four-engined Hastings. Prior to flying to Greenland experiments had been conducted at Boscombe Down commencing at 100 feet reducing at intervals to just 50 feet, quite successfully. WD492 was also specially modified for cold weather flying over Greenland where icing risks were very severe. The aircraft's de-icing system was specifically enlarged and petrol added to the engine oil to make starting easier.

On 16th September 1952, WD492 set off to supply the expedition and at 1,000 feet above the ice field roughly over the centre of Greenland the altimeter reading was 9,347 feet above sea level; i.e. the ice field at this point was 8,347 feet deep. As the Hastings descended to its drop point the pilot, in order to establish his precise altitude, relied heavily upon the aircraft's shadow over the ice, his visual horizon and radio observations from a member of the Expedition. The pilot successfully reached an altitude of 50 feet during one of its runs, when a snow or ice squall created a white out, the pilot lost his visual horizon, and the left wing tip struck the surface of the ice and snow. Despite trying to correct matters, the Hastings

Above: *Hastings C.1 TG529 of No.53 Squadron, photographed in the winter of 1953. The aircraft was en-route to the Watchfield drop-zone, Oxfordshire, carrying two Jeeps as under-slung loads on it's external heavy stores beam. See colour profile on page 83.*
Newark Air Museum

Left: *During the first half of the 1950s the majority of the Hastings fleet wore a very small squadron crest on the nose, as illustrated here on this No.511 Squadron Hastings C.2 WD488. At a later date, squadron motifs tended to be applied to the Hastings fin.*
Via David Willis/ARC

Left: *Taken at an unknown location, Hastings C.1 TG510, carrying a single code letter on the rear fuselage.*
Newark Air Museum

Royal New Zealand Air Force Hastings C.3s gained this rather more impressive bolder cheat-line along the fuselage, although at this point NZ5801 has not yet gained additional markings on the tail.
Newark Air Museum

ploughed onto the surface. Substantially intact, all 12 men aboard survived although three were injured. The Hasting's fuselage was then used by the airmen as a shelter for the following nine days before being rescued by a USAF SA-16 Albatros and a ski-equipped USAF C-47 adapted to land on ice and snow. WD492 remains in situ on the ice-cap to this day, buried under the drifting snow.

Further afield, Hastings were employed with their more-or-less routine roles most of the time. However, when conflicts involving British forces erupted, supply by air was essential and the Hastings was often called upon, it being the standard long-range RAF transport of the 1950s and early 1960s. In Africa for instance, this involved the support of the military campaign to suppress the Mau Mau uprising in Kenya. This extremist group had formed from the Kenyan African Union, who were less than happy with a lack of access to their own land and the presence of the British within their country. The situation had flared up during late 1952, when a state of emergency was declared. Matters steadily worsened throughout 1953, and with the situation deteriorating two British infantry battalions were flown into the country aboard Hastings and other chartered trooping flights during September, in a bid to halt the uprising. Hastings were also required to support RAF contingents sent to Kenya who were responsible for maintaining other RAF units equipped with Avro Lincolns and North American Harvard IIBs amongst other types. Although effectively defeated with 10,520 Mau Mau dead the Army remained in the region until 17th November 1956 after which point the uprising was deemed to be over.

Cyprus and the Suez Crisis

A little closer to the UK however, were the troubles which afflicted Cyprus from 1st April 1955 when the National Organisation of Cypriot Fighters, better known as EOKA terrorists began a bombing campaign at Larnaca, Limassol and Nicosia. A state of emergency was declared in November 1955 and lasted until December 1959. During this period another squadron began to convert to the Hastings. It would be the first Hastings unit to be based permanently away from the UK. Relinquishing its Vickers Valetta C.1s shortly after a move to Nicosia from Egypt, No.70 Squadron commenced operations in December 1955 and quickly became involved in the situation on Cyprus. EOKA struck at Nicosia in March 1956, when a bomb detonated on the base destroyed a Dakota and Hermes IV G-ALDW operated by Skyways. Whilst operations continued against the Cypriot terrorists, tensions grew between Great Britain and France on the one hand and Egypt on the other, following nationalisation of the Suez canal by the latter. This culminated in a brief war known today as the Suez Crisis in which Israel was also involved with operations against Egypt.

RAF Hastings played a large part in the Suez Crisis in October 1956, when elements of both Nos.99 and 511 Squadrons joined No.70 Squadron at Nicosia for *Operation Musketeer*. From a British perspective the air campaign commenced on 31st October 1956. The first paratroops were dropped at El Gamil airfield Egypt, on 5th November 1956 as part of *Operation Telescope*. Because the aircraft involved in the drop at El Gamil had by necessity to fly east, directly into the rising sun, many of the Hastings ground crews had covered the inside cockpit glazing with sheets of cellophane in an attempt to reduce glare. Although the drop proved to be very successful the Hastings did not emerge totally unscathed. Hastings TG612 flown by F/O A E W Waigh at an altitude of just 600 feet (this being the drop height for the paratroopers) received bullet holes through the starboard mainplane, while a Hastings from No.511 Squadron and another from

Above: *Two RNZAF Hastings C.3s on the flightline, along with several RAF examples. Note that the RAF C.2 is fitted with just two spinner caps. Hastings were often seen with either all four fitted or, more occasionally, with several removed.* Newark Air Museum

Below: *Hastings C.4 WJ324, displays both a Transport Command crest and titles on the fuselage.* Via David Willis/ARC

Above: *Hastings C.1 TG???
over El Gamil Airfield on
5th November 1965,
during the Suez Campaign.
The Hastings identity is
obscured by the
application of yellow and
black identification stripes
applied for this campaign.
It is dropping supply
canisters probably released
from the heavy lift beams
beneath the fuselage.*
Imperial War Museum

No.99 received minor flack damage. Meanwhile WD497 also from 99 Squadron, flown by F/Lt J A King DSO DFC, suffered engine problems *en route* to El Gamil caused by overheating. This resulted in the aircraft falling behind all of the other Hastings in the formation, but King pressed on regardless and dropped 14 paratroopers as well as an underslung load consisting of a Jeep and trailer and six containers. It was the presence of the underslung Jeep and trailer that caused all four engines to labour and overheat and was a common problem. This was often a factor that led to the removal of Hastings spinner caps which allowed more air to enter the air-cooled engines. Flight Lieutenant King was awarded an Air Force Cross following this incident. Incidentally, by the time of the Suez crisis the Jeep was no longer the British Army's general utility vehicle, having been replaced by the Austin Champ. However the Champ was too large to be carried externally by the Hastings so 'ancient' Jeeps were recovered from stores and, in one instance a museum, to support *Telescope*. The arrival in service of the Blackburn Beverley would overcome the need to carry such loads underslung, but in November 1956 only one squadron had as yet been equipped with the latter.

The Hastings and Valettas which participated in the drop of the 3rd Parachute Battalion Group at El Gamil had left Cyprus at 05:00 and arrived at the drop zone (DZ) at 07:15; the latter having been marked by a 139 Squadron Canberra. Prior to its arrival flak suppression sweeps by RN Seahawks and Sea Venoms and RAF Venoms had been conducted, during which the control tower was set on fire and into which sadly, one of the paratroopers fell. A second drop took place at

13:15 that day in which further troops and supplies were delivered. In total 668 paratroopers were employed. By the following day the airfield had been captured and aircraft were able to land.

The Hastings and Valettas used during *Operation Musketeer* represented virtually all of the RAF transport assets available in the region and were always in short supply, so much so that Avro Shackletons from RAF Coastal Command were often called upon to transport RAF groundcrews and additional troops to Cyprus from Britain. The Shackletons involved it was said could be later identified by the damage caused to the aircraft's floor by the soldiers hob-nail boots! No RAF transport aircraft were lost in this campaign.

Middle East and Far East confrontations

One of the longest campaigns in post-war British military history was *Operation Firedog,* which involved British and Commonwealth troops in the fight against communist guerrillas in Malaya, from 1948 to 1960. The Hastings role was unspectacular, but vital in fulfilling its principal duty of transporting men, supplies and equipment. This task was fulfiled in the main by No.48 Squadron permanently based at Changi, Singapore from 1956. Additional support was provided by the Far East Communications Squadron, also based at Changi and which operated a small flight of Hastings. As stated *Firedog* ceased in 1960 by which date only 400 to 500 terrorists remained potentially active, having retreated into remote areas of Thailand and no longer considered to be a real threat.

Another potential threat loomed in Kuwait in 1961. On 25th June 1961 the Iraqi leader arbitrarily declared that Kuwait was now part of Iraq; in similar vein to the events of nearly 30 years later. The United Kingdom immediately deployed armed forces both in support of Kuwait and to deter the implied threat of invasion by belligerent Iraqi forces. Approximately 27 Hastings, drawn from three RAF Colerne-based units: Nos. 24, 36 and 114, and No.70 Squadron from Cyprus, were deployed to transport arms and equipment to the area as swiftly as possible. By this date however, most of those troops that were transported by air were conveyed by modern RAF DH Comets and Bristol Britannias; an indication perhaps that the heyday of the Hastings was passing. The combined force of arms: Royal Navy, British Army, Royal Marines and RAF made their point; Iraqi forces did not cross into Kuwait – at least not on this occasion.

The Hastings of No.48 Squadron were also busily employed supporting ground forces during the Indonesian confrontation which had resulted from a proposal to create a Malaysian Federation. As relations deteriorated it became necessary to evacuate Britons from the Indonesian capital. A single Hastings of No.48 Squadron accompanied by three Armstrong Whitworth Argosies of No.215 Squadron were dispatched to Djakarta on 16th September 1963 and collected the evacuees.

Reorganisation

Despite the almost continuous series of crises and troubled hotspots abroad and the consequent demands made of Transport Command, the Hastings fleet in the UK continued to develop and undergo change during the 1950s. Additional squadrons were re-equipped with the Hastings while others relinquished them. Further afield, two squadrons (Nos. 48 and 70) based permanently abroad, in the Far and Middle East respectively, received Hastings in the middle of the decade. From the mid-1950s though, other more modern transport aircraft began to enter service and which would gradually replace the Hastings as a long-range transport, although its final demise in this role would not occur until January 1968. The new types were the Blackburn Beverley, Bristol Britannia, De Havilland Comet and Armstrong Whitworth Argosy. With the introduction of these later designs, several Hastings were adapted at the end of the 1950s to accommodate a further role for which they received the designation T.5. The T.5s became the last Hastings to remain in service, surviving until the 1970s.

Returning to the 1950s, May 1953 witnessed a change of base for both Nos. 24 and 47 Squadrons when they moved from Topcliffe to RAF Abingdon, Oxfordshire. Greater change within Transport Command commenced early in 1956, with the arrival of the Blackburn Beverley at Abingdon for RAF service; No.47 Squadron began converting to the Beverley during March, the first squadron to equip with this type. In contrast however, as related, No.48 Squadron, the permanent Far East unit, re-equipped with the Hastings at Changi, Singapore, during August

1956, replacing the twin-engined Valetta C.1. This Squadron's capabilities was boosted for a short period during 1959 and 60 when it received a flight of four Beverleys in order to provide a true heavy lift capability until December 1960 when the flight reformed as No.34 Squadron. (See the Beverley section within *British Military Aviation No.1* from this publisher).

Further unit changes occurred with the impending entry into service of the Bristol Britannia, which meant change within the Hasting's squadrons at RAF Lyneham, requiring No.53 Squadron to move to RAF Abingdon on 1st January 1957, where it commenced conversion to the Beverley. Both Nos. 24 and 511 Squadrons relocated to RAF Colerne, Wiltshire from Abingdon and Lyneham respectively on 1st January, although No.99 Squadron remained at Lyneham, with the Hastings for a while longer. Twenty months later, on 1st September 1958 at Colerne, No.511 Squadron disbanded although the ex-511 crews simply reformed as 36 Squadron at the same location, day and date; their previous identity being transferred to Lyneham to operate the Britannia. In January 1959, No.99 Squadron relinquished its Hastings and re-equipped with the Britannia and remained at Lyneham. Conversely, No. 114 Squadron re-formed with the Hastings as a transport unit at RAF Colerne on 5th May that year.

Ultimately, the progressive introduction of more modern aircraft and the consequent re-equipment programme created a surplus of Hastings and, although many were seconded to other duties, several more were considered to be redundant. Therefore, the opportunity was taken in 1959 to dispose of several displaced C.1s, these included TG554, 555, 558, 578, 585, 586 and TG609.

Apart from its duties within the squadrons, the Hastings was also allocated to numerous other RAF units. These included the Transport Command Development Flight, renamed the Transport Command Development Unit on 14th October 1951, based at both RAF Benson and Abingdon. This latter location also hosted the Transport Command Airborne Support Flight, which, on 14th September 1954 became 1312 Flight. The Parachute Test Unit at Henlow, Bedfordshire, also operated several Hastings. The RAF Flying College at Manby, Lincolnshire, used a pair of C.2s for training programmes that included navigational and reconnaissance flights abroad. One of their aircraft, WD499, later went on to serve with Transport Command, while the other, WJ327, was later sent to the RAE at Farnborough.

Apart from the Hastings MET.1s assigned to Coastal Command performing meteorological duties, another pair, TG618 and TG619 operated in similar fashion at Farnborough with the Meteorological Research Flight. Both aircraft assigned underwent extensive modification for the role of collecting air temperature readings, recording humidity levels, water content of clouds and noting icing conditions at low altitudes. Both aircraft were also used to fly into rainstorms to assess visibility, air turbulence and vertical currents. Other units known to have operated small numbers of Hastings include the Empire Flying School at RAF Hullavington, Wiltshire, and both the Middle East Communications Squadron (MECS) and the Far East Communications Squadron (FECS): the latter two included the use of the Hastings VIP C.4s. Number 90 Group RAF, had been renamed Signals Command on 3rd November 1958, incorporating within it the Central Signals Establishment (CSE) based at Watton, Cambridgeshire. The CSE operated a pair of Hastings, both gaining names in the process: C.1 TG560, became IRIS II (struck off charge in March 1958) and C.2 WJ338, IRIS III. Their names indicated their true purpose; radio calibration work for the Inspectorate of Radio Services. Other RAF squadrons within Signals Command used both aircraft during this period including Nos. 97, 115, 116 and 151 Squadrons. Several Hastings were also fitted for service with the Radar Reconnaissance Flight at Wyton.

Operating purely as transport aircraft to support detachments abroad, No 51 Squadron used Hastings TG507 and TG530 between 1963 and 1968.

As related, an additional role was found for a small fleet of Hastings as a consequence of the entry into RAF service, from the mid-1950s of the V-bombers, particularly (at a later date) the Avro Vulcan. Bomber Command required a replacement for the Avro Lincoln which was, in the 1950s, used to conduct the training of crews destined to operate the radar and electronic equipment fitted to the V-bombers. Hastings TG503, loaned to the TRE at Defford as early as January 1951, had been fitted with H2S Mk9 ground-mapping radar in a radome fitted under the fuselage. Once the trials had been successfully completed, TG503 was delivered to the Bomber Command Bombing School based at RAF Lindholme, South Yorkshire, gaining the designation Hastings T.5 in the process. A contract for a further seven airframe conversions was awarded to Airwork Limited at Blackbushe. The major changes incorporated a training station for the H2S operator in the fuselage which in turn was sited above a new ventral radome. The rear of the aircraft retained a passenger and cargo carrying capability for secondary support work within Bomber Command. Several of the airframes chosen for conversion were serving with No.202 Squadron as MET.1s, including TG517. The other six were: TG505, 511, 518, 521, 529 and TG553. TG505 underwent further trials with the A&AEE from 1st January 1960 and, as further deliveries were made, the BCBS began to retire those Lincolns which remained in the training role. The last delivery occurred during February 1962 after a short period in storage. It is perhaps an irony that the Lincolns were replaced by an aircraft every bit as old as they were; although the suitability of the Hastings capacious fuselage by comparison with the Lincoln cannot be doubted.

Hastings with the RNZAF

The four aircraft purchased by the RNZAF, were allocated initially to No.41 Squadron from November 1952, with the fourth aircraft, NZ5804 being the last new Hastings built. It was entered into the London to Christchurch air race, though unfortunately suffered an engine failure inbound to Negombo, Ceylon, during a severe tropical storm. The aircraft suffered damage while landing on the flooded runway and was forced into an early withdrawal from the race. Once repaired NZ5804 returned to New Zealand although its subsequent flying career was cut short in a crash landing at Darwin Airport, leaving the RNZAF with a fleet of only three Hastings which performed regular flights to and from the UK. No.41 Squadron also performed regular supply flights to the Chatham and Fiji Island chains, as well as supporting a detachment of RNZAF units to Cyprus. The aircraft had also participated in a number of support duties including the support of 'K' Force in Japan between 1954 and 1956, ferrying both troops and their equipment. 'K' Force was a part of New Zealands contribution to the UN forces maintained in theatre as a result of the earlier Korean War.

In December 1954 No.41 was renumbered No.40 Squadron RNZAF and the three remaining Hastings were returned to the UK for a main spar replacement during 1961, to extend their working lives. From mid-1964 these Hastings were employed on logistical flights from New Zealand to Vietnam in support of their troops deployed there. They were supported by No.41 Squadron, by this time equipped with the Bristol Freighter.

The RNZAF finally retired NZ5802 and 5803 at Whenuapai during May 1965, before their transfer to Ohakea for storage in February 1966. They were joined by NZ5801, which performed the last flight of the type on 2nd February 1966.

Today, the only surviving sections of an RNZAF Hastings is the forward fuselage and several smaller parts from NZ5801, retained at the Museum of Transport and Technology (MOTAT) in Auckland, on North Island.

Opposite page:

Top: *Transport Command Hastings often wore the Transport Command Badge, visible on the nearest aircraft beneath the cockpit.* David Willis/ARC

Bottom: *Towards the end of the 1950s a relaxation of fleet-wide pooling meant that each Hastings squadron could add a little colour to their aircraft. Illustrated here is C.2 WD491, assigned to No.53 Squadron based at RAF Lyneham, with the Squadron number within the diamond displayed on the fin.* Newark Air Museum

This page from top:

TG616 illustrates the non-jettisonable external fuel tanks fitted as part of the C.1A conversion programme.

At this stage the majority of the RAF Hastings fleet still retained silver fins as in this image taken in 1956, depicting TG615 of 1312 Flight based at RAF Abingdon. This aircraft crashed at RAF Colerne on 21st October 1957.

TG513 of No.242 Operational Conversion Unit wore a red and yellow diamond with white and black characters on the fin.

The Hastings MET.1s of No.202 Squadron opted initially for an overall Dark Sea Grey scheme. Some carried a yellow cheat-line, together with a yellow circle on the tail with red figures 202 within. The circle was repeated on the nose, with a single letter code. In this instance 'R' is just discernable on TG567's nose in 1957. All Newark Air Museum

Opposite page:

Top: *WJ334 a C.2 of No.36 Squadron, date unknown, but post September 1958 when 36 Squadron reformed from No.511 Squadron at RAF Colerne.* David Willis/ARC

Bottom: *The Royal New Zealand Air Force Hastings C.3s were regular visitors to the UK throughout their service career. NZ5802 is seen at Northolt on 25th June 1964 with the later RNZAF titles and the City of Auckland crest on the fin.* Richard L Ward

Above: *Hastings C.1 TG607 No.24 Squadron, at RAF Colerne.*
David Willis/ARC

Below: *The principal external difference between the Hastings C.1 and C.2 may be discerned in this view, i.e. the relative positions of the tailplane. Furthest from the camera is C.1 TG605 of No.114 Squadron, whilst the nearer of the two is C.2 WD477 of No.36 Squadron. They are seen together over Mount Kilimanjaro.* via David Willis/ARC

Above: Hastings C.2 WJ327 of No.36 Squadron, using outboard engines only taxies past Blackburn Beverley XM105 from No.30 Squadron. WJ327 displays the Squadron motif on its fin: an eagle carrying a torpedo, a reference to an earlier bygone Squadron role. Brandon White

Left: Hastings C.1A TG531 from No.48 Squadron between missions. This Squadron was one of the resident Hastings units at RAF Changi, Singapore. The other unit was the Far East Communications Squadron that existed for a time during the 1950s. Newark Air Museum

Left: Photographed at Darwin, Australia in 1956, the first production RNZAF Hastings C.3 carries the Transport wing titles within the upper fuselage trim. via Richard L Ward

Left: Hastings C.1 TG533 illustrates the two-coloured diamond worn by No. 242 OCU.
Adrian Balch Archive

Below: C.1A TG607 from No.242 OCU, minus the diamond motif, seen at Waterbeach in September 1961, with a Vickers Valiant behind. Richard L Ward

Bottom: Hastings C.1A TG570 was serving with No.242 OCU during September 1963. This image was taken while the aircraft was on a visit to RAF Wattisham.
Richard L Ward

Above: *The final variant of the Hastings to receive a new mark number was the T.5 for the Bomber Command Bombing School based for most of its life at RAF Lindholme. All were conversions of existing airframes. This image of TG511 illustrates the first colour scheme adopted by the Hastings of that unit; silver with a yellow band around the rear fuselage and wings.* Handley Page Association

Below: *T.5 TG553 at RAF Lindholme in October 1961. This image quite clearly shows the yellow training band applied around the rear fuselage and to each wing between the two engines. The other yellowish lines appear to be exhaust stains.* Newark Air Museum

Above: Hastings T.5 *TG521 of the BCBS at RAF Lindholme. A yellow training band can be partially seen on the leading edge of the starboard wing between the engines. See profile page 89.* Newark Air Museum

Below: *Yellow training bands were later replaced by the liberal application of Day-Glo, as seen here on TG505 at Lindholme.* Richard L Ward

Above: *BCBS T.5 TG521 landing at Odiham on 10th September 1964, gives a good indication of the generous application of Day-Glo.* Richard L Ward

Below: *Hastings T.5, TG518 is seen during its early days after conversion and was photographed in the static park at the RAF Waddington airshow in September 1962. See 4-view on page 90 and 91.* Newark Air Museum

Chapter 5: **TOWARDS RETIREMENT**

The 1960s saw the Hastings enter its final decade of large scale service with the RAF. At the beginning of that decade it still served with three transport squadrons: Nos. 24, 36 and 114 at RAF Colerne, as well as 242 OCU, which moved from RAF Dishforth to Thorney Island Hampshire, in February 1962. Additionally, No.202 Squadron continued with the Hastings at Aldergrove, as well as Nos. 48 and 70 abroad. Several aircraft were also in use with other, smaller units within the UK. The arrival of the Armstrong Whitworth Argosy into RAF service reduced the Colerne based Hastings squadrons to two, when No.114 Squadron disbanded on 30th September 1961. The remaining MET.1s continued to serve No.202 Squadron, with TG565 serving at the A&AEE during 1963 to trial an Ekco designed, cloud and collision weather warning radar. It later returned to No.202 Squadron. Ultimately, changes within Coastal Com-

The End of Transport Command

As the 1960s progressed, further reductions of the Hastings fleet continued with the disbandment of No.242 OCU, early in 1967. The next unit to disband was No.48 Squadron at Changi on 3rd March 1967, followed shortly by one of the remaining Colerne Wing squadrons, No.36 during July. No. 36 converted to the Lockheed Hercules soon afterwards at RAF Lyneham. In Cyprus, No.70 Squadron moved to nearby Akrotiri in 1966, as part of the Near East Air Force, Cyprus. The NEAF had been formed on 1st March 1961; having formally been the Middle East Air Force at the same location. The unit re-equipped with the Argosy in November 1967, although it retained a Hastings C.4 until July 1968. The final UK-based Hastings squadron was No.24, which also re-equipped with the Hercules from 5th January 1968.

On 1st of August 1967, RAF Transport Command

Hastings C.1A TG533 of No.242 OCU at Thorney Island, note that the aircraft wears its radio callsign MOGCB in small letters on the nose radome. Via Ray Sturtivant

mand and improvements in weather forecasting techniques spelt the end for 202 Squadron's Meteorological role, and it disbanded at Aldergrove on 31st July 1964.

During this period, however, it proved necessary to ground the entire remaining Hastings fleet following the loss of TG577 from 36 Squadron near Abingdon on 6th July 1965. Of all the accidents that the Hastings suffered during its long service career, this ranked as the worst. The cause was due to fatigue within the upper bolts that attached the elevator to the tailplane, which fractured shortly after take-off. The crew of six and 35 RAF and Army parachutists were all killed. As a result of this accident all Hastings underwent inspection, the tail unit and elevators were refurbished by a combination of RAF and Handley Page working parties at home and abroad.

was re-titled RAF Air Support Command until integrated into RAF Strike Command on 1st September 1972. (Strike Command had been formed on 30th April 1968, by merging both Bomber and Fighter Commands). Following the retirement of most of the Hastings fleet, redundant Hastings were flown to various locations for storage, pending disposal or allocated to numerous airfields and other establishments for fire practice. Despite the end of transport operations there remained two Hastings with the RAE, two with the MRF at Farnborough and several in use with the A&AEE. Following the retirement of the Hermes II, VX234, the RRE at Pershore required a replacement trials aircraft and received Hastings C.2, WD499. The last remaining aircraft with Signals Command, WJ338, was finally retired on 4th July 1969. With the formation of Strike Command, the Bomber Command Bombing School at RAF Lindholme amended its title slightly to

Above: *Passengers board C.1 TG527, with engines running. The Day-Glo applied to the nose and tail has weathered significantly.* Newark Air Museum

Below: *A pair of Hastings C.1As from No.48 Squadron overflying the jungle somewhere in the Far East. Note that TG525 has had its spinner caps removed whereas TG523 retains them.* Newark Air Museum

become the Strike Command Bombing School (SCBS). In addition to the T.5s with which it was equipped, the unit gained a pair of C.1As to perform its own aircrew conversion training. One of these spent only a short time with the SCBS, and so another C.1A, TG568, was procured to operate alongside TG536 and the eight T.5s. Three T.5s were soon disposed of however, with two going in 1969 and another in 1971.

The SCBS moved from RAF Lindholme to RAF Scampton Lincolnshire, on 1st September 1972, changing its name to the Hastings Radar Flight in the process. On 1st January 1974, the HRF was placed under the control of No.230 OCU. The Flight also assumed responsibility for the training of Hawker Siddeley Buccaneer and McDonnell Douglas F-4 Phantom FG.1 and FGR.2 navigators, in addition to those from the Vulcan squadrons. During this period the Flight gained the unofficial nickname '1066 Squadron' whilst stationed at RAF Scampton.

Several of those Hastings operated by the A&AEE at Boscombe Down and the RAE at Farnborough survived until finally retired in the early 1970s. At Boscombe Down, TG502 flew until it was retired in 1972, followed by TG500 a year later. The pair of C.2s operated by the RAE and the RRE were finally retired in August and September 1974, WD480 flew for the last time on 21st August, and WD499 made its final flight on the 30th September

The Cod War

An additional responsibility acquired by the Hastings Radar Flight was to patrol the offshore oil-rigs in the North Sea. An extension of this maritime duty required the Hastings to perform its last ever operational duty; reconnaissance for the protection of the British fishing fleet during the infamous fishing dispute between the UK and Iceland. Known as the third 'Cod War', it took place during the autumn and winter of 1975/76. The Hastings also dropped supplies to warships of the Royal Navy during *Operation Heliotrope*, (the code name given to the Royal Navy's involvement). Hastings are known to have made at least 20 sorties during this period, in addition to the 158 sorties conducted by BAe Nimrods. The Hastings' involved were adorned with suitable Day-Glo cod fish symbols on the nose for each mission.

In preservation

Hastings C.1A, TG528 was purchased by the Skyfame museum and flown into Staverton airport, Gloucestershire, in January 1968. It remained there until the museum closed in 1978, however the Imperial War Museum managed to save TG528 and had it dismantled and transferred to Duxford in the spring of 1979. Following reassembly the aircraft stood outside for over 20 years, undergoing a refurbishment during the mid-1980s with a second restoration that commenced in 2006, prior to entering the new Airspace hanger in the spring of 2007. It is now painted to represent its early service days when it performed duties during the Berlin Airlift.

Elements of C.1A TG536 survive albeit as part of a Halifax restoration. TG536 was originally flown to RAF Colerne after retirement from the SCBS, and kept in their museum collection until its eventual closure. This aircraft was one of the few deemed surplus to requirements, as a consequence of which it was transferred to the Fire School at Catterick North Yorkshire. TG536 managed to escape the cutters torch for a few more years. Meanwhile the Yorkshire Air Museum, at Elvington airfield near York, were in the process of constructing a replica Halifax, a composite of several airframes. The inner wing sections, undercarriage and certain other components of TG536 were purchased for use in the Halifax replica.

When 230 OCU finally retired its last four Hastings, three of them were saved for posterity.

TG517 was flown to the Newark Air Museum at Winthorpe airfield, Nottinghamshire on 22nd June 1977. The airframe still survives to this day, although currently kept outside, plans to house the aircraft indoors were revealed in March 2007.

TG503 was retired a week later and flown to RAF Gatow on 29th June, where it initially served as a memorial at the base to commemorate the Berlin Airlift. It remained there until gifted to the Deutsches Historiches Museum on the 11th July 1994, although the aircraft remained at Gatow until 21st September 1997. On this date the aircraft was moved to the Alliierten Museum (Allied Museum) in Berlin. Part of the journey was conducted by airlift utilising a Mil Mi-26 Halo heavylift helicopter. All four engines had to be removed as were the wings outboard of the two inner engines. The remainder of the journey was completed by road and on arrival at its new location the airframe was reassembled, and refurbished with help from the RAF.

TG511 was the last Hastings to enter retirement and is credited with being the last Hastings to fly. It was flown to RAF Cosford, to become a part of the Aerospace Museum; TG511 was ultimately moved into the National Cold War Exhibition during 2006.

TG505 was the fourth Hastings and did not survive into preservation. This Hastings was flown to St Athan and later moved by road to Ewyas Harold, Herefordshire for use at the Pontrilas Army Training Area, as a training aid by the SAS.

C.2 WD479 of No.48 Squadron. The rear under fuselage access door, just left of the ladder is open. Via Ray Sturtivant

Towards the end of their service life the Hastings MET.1s of 202 Squadron lost their overall Dark Sea Grey colour scheme when the fuselage upper surfaces were painted white. TG567 has a demarcation line similar to the cheat-line generally seen on transport Hastings. Newark Air Museum

MET.1 TG624 also received a white fuselage topside. In this instance however the demarcation line is different from that of TG567. Newark Air Museum

C.1A TG612 of No.48 Squadron. Bristol Belvedere HC.1 helicopters can be seen in the far distance behind 612's tailplane.
Brandon White

C.1A TG527 at RAF Colerne in September 1965. The aircraft has had its fin and tailplanes removed, most likely as a direct consequence of the fatal accident that befell TG577 during July of that year, which necessitated an inspection of every Hastings tailplane.
Brandon White

Occasionally the Hastings Squadrons performed formation flypasts. Five aircraft of No.48 Squadron are seen here on 7th December 1965. The Squadron Commander subsequently apologised for the small number of aircraft involved; caused by others having been seconded elsewhere.
Via David Willis/ARC

Above: *With their flypast complete all five No.48 Squadron Hastings taxi back to the flightline at RAF Changi.* Newark Air Museum

Below: *No.70 Squadron were part of the RAF Near East Air Force, and were regular visitors to RAF Luqa, better known today as Malta International Airport. Hastings C.2, WJ328 is seen there on 6th March 1966.* Newark Air Museum

Above: *TG568 is seen at the Handley Page airfield, Radlett, Hertfordshire. Date unknown.*
Brandon White

Right and below right: *Towards the end of their service career, the last two Squadrons at Colerne equipped with Hastings applied their Squadron motifs to the fins of their aircraft, as illustrated here. The image on the right illustrates No.24 Squadron's Blackcock painted on C.2 WJ340, while below right WD491 displays the No.36 Squadron Eagle motif carrying a torpedo. Remnants of badly worn Day-Glo are evident.*
Both Newark Air Museum

Left: *Hastings C.2 WD499, of No.36 Squadron. This aircraft later went on to serve with the Royal Radar Establishment at Pershore.* Ray Sturtivant

Below: *The last operational RAF Hastings squadron was No.24. Hastings C.2 WJ340 is seen bearing the title of Transport Command's successor, which was worn for a relatively short period. No.24 Squadron re-equipped with the Hercules from January 1968, and WJ340 was struck off charge the following month.* Newark Air Museum

Above: *Hastings T.5 TG521 seen flying from RAF Lindholme during its days with the Strike Command Bombing School. The aircraft is flying over one of several coal-fired power stations that are sited near the River Trent on the Lincolnshire and Nottinghamshire county border.*

Right: *In the shadow of Beverley XH124 is Hastings C.1A TG527, at Abingdon for the 50th Anniversary of the RAF in 1968. This Hastings had earlier been allocated, very briefly, to the Bomber Command, later Strike Command Bombing School. It was replaced by TG568. Both Newark Air Museum*

Left: *Former SCBS Hastings T.5 TG518, seen shortly after its arrival at Carlisle airport on 13th May 1969. It had been struck off charge on the same day to become a fire training airframe.* Newark Air Museum

Centre: *Hastings C.1 TG605 of No.24 Squadron.* Richard L Ward

Below: *C.1A TG526 with TG523 behind at RAF Changi in April 1966. TG526 has had all four spinner caps removed, while TG523 retains them. The red equilateral triangle on the fin forms part of No.48 Squadron's Badge. This motif (i.e. the triangle) was applied to the tail with the number '48' set within it, as opposed to the original Squadron Badge which displayed the head of a petrel within the triangle.* Adrian Balch Archive

Opposite page:

Top: *Hastings C.1A TG606 of No.70 Squadron, based at RAF Akrotiri, seen cruising over Cyprus shortly before the unit retired its Hastings and converted to the Argosy.*
Adrian Balch Archive

Centre: *Remembrance Day Colerne, November 1967 with some of No.24 Squadron's last operational Hastings.*
Adrian Balch Archive

Bottom: *The second production Hastings C.1 (later C.1A) TG500.*
Richard L Ward

Top: *Hastings C.2 WJ338 IRIS III of RAF Signals Command during a visit to RAF Odiham in September 1968. See colour profile on page 87.*

Centre: *Hastings C.1A TG568 of the Strike Command Bombing School makes an impressive sight on departure from RAF Lyneham in May 1972.*

Bottom: *Hastings C.2 WJ327 is seen taking off during one of the SBAC trade show and air displays held at Farnborough. This was one of the few un-modified Hastings operated by the RAE.*
All Adrian Balch Archive

Chapter 6: **HASTINGS IN DETAIL**

This chapter is included to illustrate selected details of the Hastings T.5 TG517, now preserved at the Newark Air Museum, on the former airfield at Winthorpe near Newark, Nottinghamshire.

By the beginning of 2008 TG517 had stood outside for 30 years, and has faired relatively well in the harsh UK climate, and remains in remarkably good condition. TG517 was built as a C.1 before conversion to a MET.1 with Coastal Command to operate over the North Atlantic. It was later converted to a T.5.

Opposite page left, this page above left and right: *Three views inside the cockpit of TG517, offering a general idea of the insrument layout. The two blue plastic buckets act as a modern day concession to the now less than watertight nature of the cockpit glazing.*

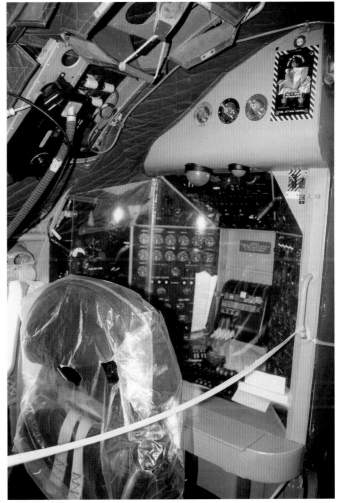

Above left and right: *Crew stations for the navigator (left), and flight engineer (right). In both instances a Perspex protective screen is in place.*

Top right, far right and centre left: *Visible on either side of the nose are the Rebecca receiver aerials together with the larger trailing aerial mast. Also of interest is the bomb aimer-style windows sometimes used when dropping supplies. The nose entry access hatch is just behind.*

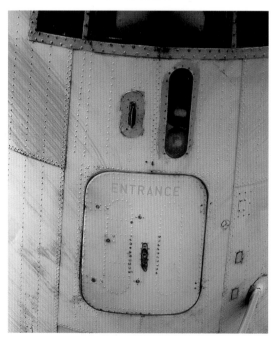

Centre right and bottom right: *While moving around the starboard side of the airframe a look at the wing section reveals how close the tips of both propellers are. Also of note are the injection air intakes on the left of each engine when looking from head on, and the oil cooler intakes on the right.*

Far left and left: *Three photographs of the starboard main landing gear leg strut and wheel together with the undercarriage doors and the Hercules engine nacelles.*

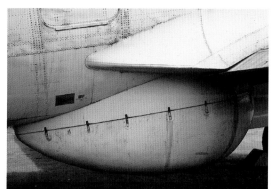

Far left: *A general view of the engine nacelles on the starboard wing.*

Left: *Moving towards the rear of the airframe aft of the engines reveals the aft wingroot fillet and the radome as fitted to the T.5. Also, just visible is the starboard passenger/ paratroop door.*

Far left: *Retractable tail wheel and associated doors.*

Left: *Visible below the cockpit are the mission symbols gained during the Cod war.*

Chapter 7: **HASTINGS COLOURS**

After the Second World War, most Transport Command aircraft were repainted in High Speed Silver, previously identified as High Gloss Aluminium, (see full explanation on page 76). All early RAF Hastings C.1s and some of the early C.2s were delivered in overall High Speed Silver. Upon entry into service they gained a dark blue cheat-line running the length of the fuselage.

During 1951, the Hastings transport fleet underwent its first repaint, which included the addition of white fuselage topsides. The remainder of the airframe retained High Speed Silver, including the fin and rudder. The fuselage cheat-line acted as the demarcation line between the two. Both of these colour schemes were evident during the Coronation Review of the RAF at RAF Odiham in 1953. During the Suez campaign in 1956, most of the participating Hastings carried yellow and black invasion identification stripes around the fuselage and wings.

Squadron markings usually consisted, initially, of a standard Transport Command diamond on top of the fin with the squadron number within, usually in white. At a later stage squadrons began to use different colours for the fin diamonds, although in No.48 Squadron's instance they replaced the diamond with a triangle. Most Hastings had small black serials on the fuselage, repeated under the wings, with the last three numerals being displayed on the fin. During the Berlin Airlift several Hastings employed the complete serial on the fin with the two letters displayed slightly smaller, set above the rest of the serial. It would seem that in some instances this arrangement was retained for a considerable period beyond the Airlift. Most of the aircraft involved on Airlift duties also carried a single letter code on the rear fuselage aft of the freight doors.

A variation within the Hastings fleet during the 1950s was the employment by a few Hastings squadrons of a three letter code on the fuselage. This was in fact the last three letters of the aircraft's callsign, the last letter however was the aircraft's individual identification letter. With the addition of white fuselage topsides the fleet also carried titles denoting to whom the aircraft was allocated, e.g. Transport Command or in the case of overseas based squadrons, Far East, Near East or Middle East Air Force titles. These titles were often accompanied by two small flashes above one another at each end of the title. During the early years of service the majority of the aircraft also carried a squadron crest although this was usually very small, and appeared on the nose near the cockpit glazing. The Hastings prototypes carried the standard ringed yellow 'P' denoting its prototype status.

Towards the end of the service career of the Hastings, as a transport, and with the demise of Transport Command itself, a few surviving aircraft received RAF Air Support Command titles instead. These were applied to the fuselage in lieu of the previous title 'Transport Command'.

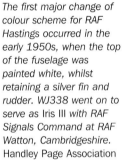

The first major change of colour scheme for RAF Hastings occurred in the early 1950s, when the top of the fuselage was painted white, whilst retaining a silver fin and rudder. WJ338 went on to serve as Iris III with RAF Signals Command at RAF Watton, Cambridgeshire.
Handley Page Association

Two views of the second Hastings C.3 NZ5802 for the Royal New Zealand Air Force. Seen at Radlett immediately prior to its delivery flight, this aircraft illustrates the thin demarcation line applied to separate white from silver along the fuselage centre line. Cocooned Hastings can be seen in storage in the distance in the bottom photograph.
Handley Page Association

The Colour Silver!

During WW2 and the early post war period many RAF aircraft received a partial or overall coat of aluminium paint. In recent times confusion has arisen between the application of aluminium or silver paint.

In January 1953 an internal Air Ministry memo AMOA.658/52 dated 18th December 1952 was circulated stating that the previously referred to colour aluminium would be referred to from that point as High Speed Silver. This is the earliest reference to High Speed Silver as opposed to its previous name aluminium. Later, in January 1953, a Ministry of Supply memo stated that in all such references the word silver was to replace aluminium and the words High Speed were to replace High Gloss, which was often used as a prefix to aluminium. Ergo: same paint and finish just a different name.

With regard to references throughout this book the term High Speed Silver has sometimes simply been referred to as silver!

The Hastings MET.1s of No.202 Squadron, Coastal Command, were painted in a different colour scheme, initially appearing with Medium Sea Grey topsides and white undersides. The aircraft were allocated codes with the prefix 'Y3' although this later changed to two letter codes with the prefix 'A'. Their original colour scheme was soon replaced with an overall Dark Sea Grey pattern which incorporated a white cheat-line, although evidence exists to suggest that the cheat-line was painted yellow in some instances. With the repainting of its aircraft in this latter scheme, No.202 Squadron initially carried a white disc on the top of the fin with the squadron numbers in red within, together with white Coastal Command titles. Presumably the disc would be rendered in yellow to match the yellow cheat-line if appropriate. (Please refer to colour artwork). Eventually the MET.1s were repainted to receive white fuselage tops. Later, the large squadron number '202' was adopted and displayed in red with a white outline on the fuselage. With this later scheme the unit often applied single letter codes on the nose tip and the squadrons mallard motif on the fin.

Royal New Zealand Air Force Hastings C.3s were completed with a similar basic colour scheme to that of RAF Transport Command: white fuselage tops, fin, rudder and High Speed Silver for the remainder of the airframe. Beyond that however, the RNZAF Hastings became distinctly different. During the early 1950s, they initially carried a very thin cheat-line along the length of the fuselage, later changed to a much broader blue cheat-line. RNZAF Hastings initially carried standard RAF type 'D' roundels and fin flash, although later the silver fern national symbol was added to the centre of each roundel.

VIP Hastings C.4s also carried a bolder and straighter cheat-line than the one that appeared on the RAF transport versions, although variations appeared later.

Bomber Command Bombing School Hastings were initially painted in the standard RAF training scheme of overall High Speed Silver, with yellow training bands around the wings and rear fuselage. The H2S radome was black. The yellow was later removed and Day-Glo orange liberally applied to the airframe, particularly to the fin, nose, tailplanes and wingtips. At a later stage some of the surviving T.5s were repainted acquiring white fuselage tops whilst retaining silver wings and undersurfaces. Later still, a few received an application of Light Aircraft Grey to replace the silver. The T.5s operated by No.230 OCU had their Day-Glo replaced with red paint and the radome eventually painted Light Aircraft Grey.

As related elsewhere individual or small groups of Hastings continued to serve with several small units or other establishments. Their colour schemes varied considerably, often on an individual basis, several of these schemes may be examined in colour photographs and artwork within this book.

Above right: An early photograph of IRIS III, the second Hastings to carry the IRIS name while assigned to RAF Signals Command. Hastings C.2, WJ338 wears the thicker yellow cheat-line seen during January 1964. Adrian Balch Archive

Right: A close up view of the weather radar nose fitted to A&AEE Hastings C.1A TG500. Richard L Ward

BOSCOMBE DOWN

Top: *Hastings MET.1 TG565 in May 1962, Bovingdon. Coastal Command Hastings wore this Dark Sea Grey and White colour scheme in the later years of service. They also bore the large style squadron number on the fuselage similar to those displayed by Avro Shackletons of the era.* Tony Eastwood collection

Above: *Hastings C.1 TG509 of No.70 Squadron undergoing maintenance at Sharjah in 1966; the port inner propeller has been removed. The Squadron diamond on the tail (seen above right) had by this time been replaced by the Squadron motif; a demi-winged lion.* Adrian Balch Archive

Above: *Hastings C.1 TG561 of No.70 Squadron at Sharjah in May 1964. The familiar Transport Command diamond motif contains the Squadron number LXX.* Adrian Balch Archive

Below: *Hastings C.2 WJ336 was attached to the Far East Air Force Communications Flight and is seen here during a visit to Richmond Australia during December 1966. Of interest is the inscription CAL 1 just below the cockpit.* Adrian Balch Archive

Three images of the heavily modified RAE Hastings C.2 WD480. See 4-view on page 92/93.

Top: *March 1969. Close examination of this photograph shows the engine nacelles to be painted the same shade of blue as the spinner caps; at a later date the nacelles were painted black.* Newark Air Museum

Centre: *Abingdon in September 1973 shows the size of the pannier fitted for sonobuoy trials.* Mick Freer via Adrian Balch

Below: *Landing at Boscombe Down in February 1973.* Adrian Balch

Opposite page:

Top: *Hastings C.4 WD500. Towards the end of its life it was assigned to the Akrotiri Station Flight and gained a cheat-line lower than that on any other Hastings. It would appear that WD500 has been finished in overall Light Aircraft Grey with a white fuselage top, fin and rudder, with a blue cheat-line. The badge on the fin is that of the NEAF. The name Hibernia appears below the cockpit.* Adrian Balch archive

Centre: *Complete with Air Support Command titles, TG621 is seen on the ramp at Lyneham on 9th March 1968. The aircraft still wears the motif of the last transport squadron to operate the Hastings.* Tony Eastwood Collection

Bottom: *Hastings C.2 WJ339 of No.36 Squadron. One of the last operational Hastings units, re-equipping in July 1967. WJ339 is seen taxiing at RAF Gaydon, Warwickshire. The shield beneath the cockpit is the motif extracted from the City of Bath Coat of Arms.* Richard L Ward

Opposite page:

Top: *Hastings C.2 WD496, operated by the A&AEE at Boscombe Down. After being retired the aircraft spent its final years on the fire dump at Boscombe Down finally being removed in July 1989. Note the nose probe and faded roundels. See profile on page 87. Adrian Balch collection*

Bottom: *Hastings T.5 TG503 taxiing out for take-off at RAF Coningsby during the summer of 1976. Terry Senior*

Top: *Hastings T.5 TG517 of No.230 OCU based at RAF Scampton, displaying its four Cod War symbols. This aircraft is now preserved at the Newark Air Museum. Denis Calvert*

Bottom: *Also bearing four Cod War symbols, Hastings T.5 TG505 astride the cross runway at Coningsby in March 1977. TG505 was the only one of the last four remaining Hastings T.5s that did not survive into preservation. No doubt it proved its worth in its final years as a training aid with the SAS. Terry Senior*

C.1

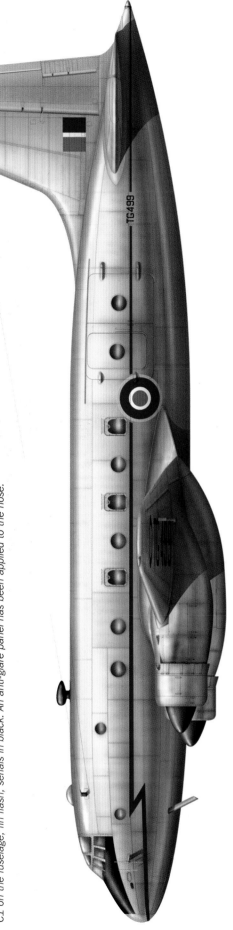

Hastings C.1, TG499. *Painted in the early overall silver colour scheme with a standard Transport Command dark blue cheat-line. The aircraft wears Type C roundels above and below the wings, type C1 on the fuselage; fin flash, serials in black. An anti-glare panel has been applied to the nose.*

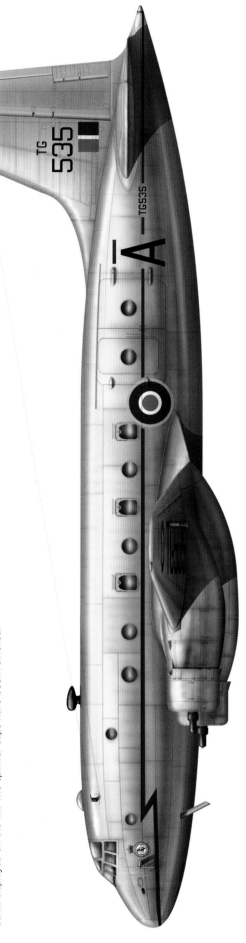

Hastings C.1, TG535. *As seen during the Berlin Airlift, standard overall silver with blue cheat-line. Type C and C1 roundels as per TG499 above; fin flash, black serials and codes, with the entire serial displayed on the fin. The spinner caps have been removed.*

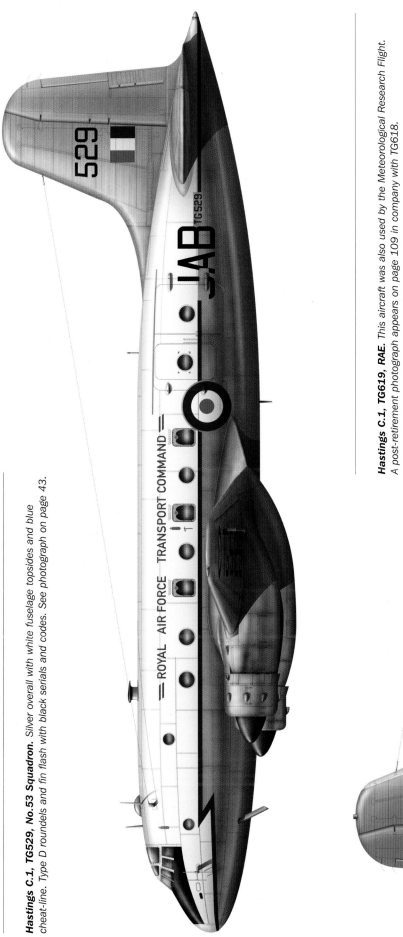

Hastings C.1, TG529, No.53 Squadron. Silver overall with white fuselage topsides and blue cheat-line. Type D roundels and fin flash with black serials and codes. See photograph on page 43.

Hastings C.1, TG619, RAE. This aircraft was also used by the Meteorological Research Flight. A post-retirement photograph appears on page 109 in company with TG618.

Hastings TG502. Something of a hybrid, this aircraft was built as a C.1 and used to test a modified and lowered tailplane (seen here) later employed on the production C.2, C.3 and C.4. TG502 is fitted with the underwing fuel tanks employed on the C.1A as part of the C.1 upgrade programme. TG502 was utilised by the A&AEE, Boscombe Down, throughout most of its life. Illustrated here as it appeared in the early 1970s; overall Light Aircraft Grey, white fuselage topsides, bold red cheat-line with black outlines. The fin was painted Roundel Red which replaced the earlier Day-Glo. Type D roundels and fin flash with black serials.

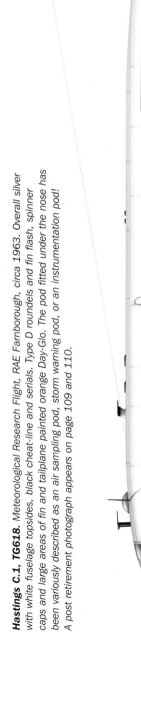

Hastings C.1, TG618. Meteorological Research Flight, RAE Farnborough, circa 1963. Overall silver with white fuselage topsides, black cheat-line and serials. Type D roundels and fin flash, spinner caps and large areas of fin and tailplane painted orange Day-Glo. The pod fitted under the nose has been variously described as an air sampling pod, storm warning pod, or an instrumentation pod! A post retirement photograph appears on page 109 and 110.

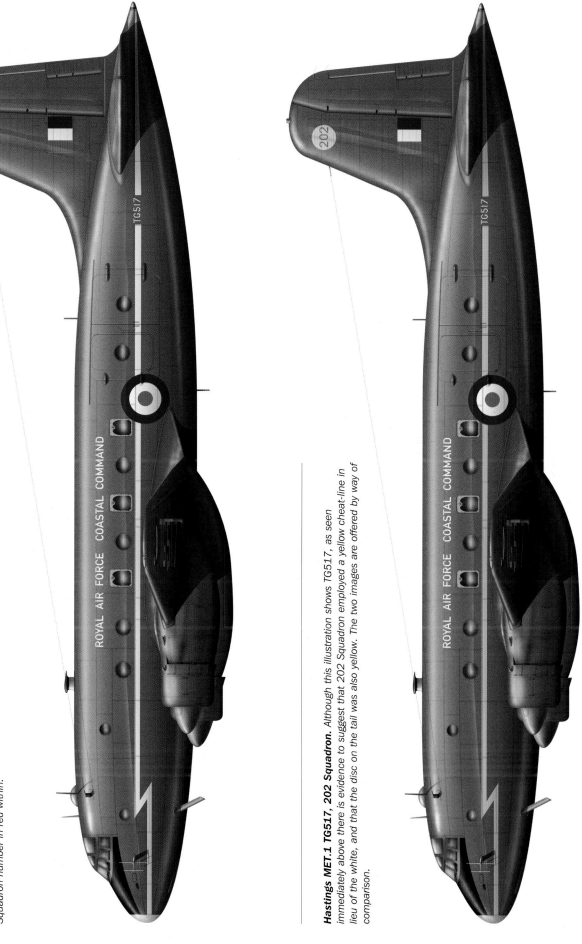

MET.1

Hastings MET.1 TG517, 202 Squadron. *Dark Sea Grey overall with white serials white cheat-line with full RAF Coastal Command titles in white. Type D roundels and fin flash, white circle on fin with Squadron number in red within.*

Hastings MET.1 TG517, 202 Squadron. *Although this illustration shows TG517, as seen immediately above there is evidence to suggest that 202 Squadron employed a yellow cheat-line in lieu of the white, and that the disc on the tail was also yellow. The two images are offered by way of comparison.*

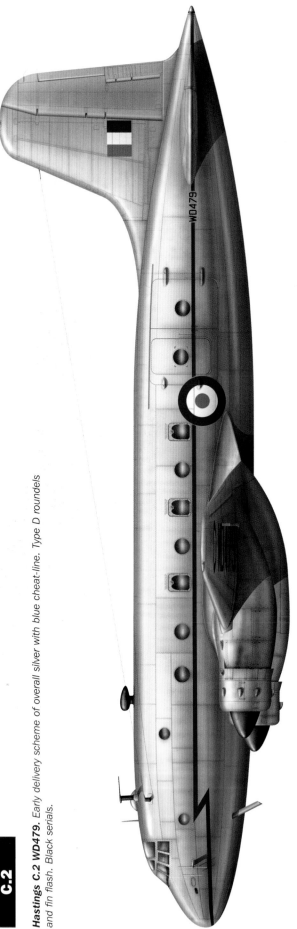

C.2

Hastings C.2 WD479. Early delivery scheme of overall silver with blue cheat-line. Type D roundels and fin flash. Black serials.

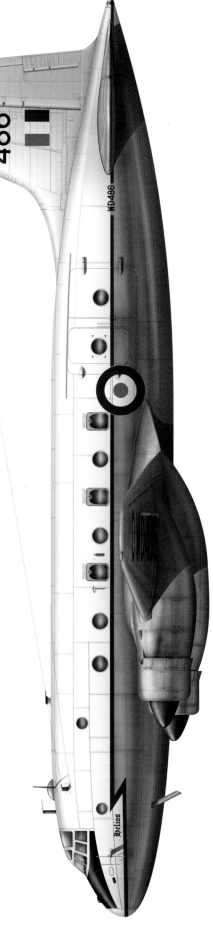

Hastings C.2 WD486, 70 Squadron. Silver overall with white fuselage topsides, fin and rudder. The name Helios was applied to both sides below the cockpit with the squadron motif appearing on the fin with the Roman numerals LXX below. Type D roundels and fin flash, black serials and codes. Helios was the Greek sun god who drove his golden chariot across the sky from east to west every day!

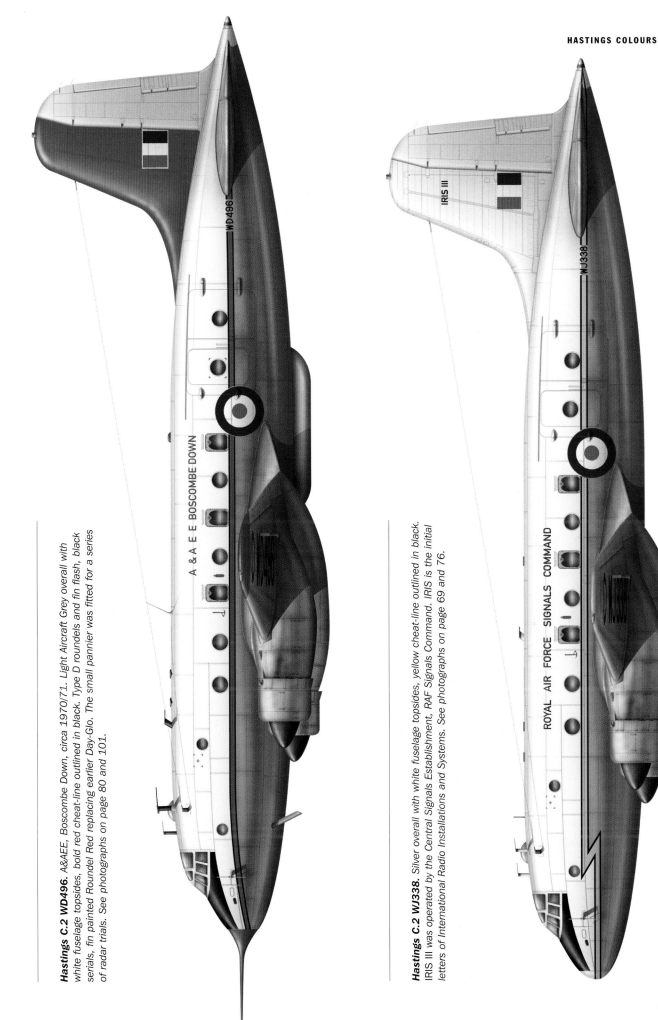

Hastings **C.2 WD496.** A&AEE, Boscombe Down, circa 1970/71. Light Aircraft Grey overall with white fuselage topsides, bold red cheat-line outlined in black. Type D roundels and fin flash, black serials, fin painted Roundel Red replacing earlier Day-Glo. The small pannier was fitted for a series of radar trials. See photographs on page 80 and 101.

Hastings **C.2 WJ338.** Silver overall with white fuselage topsides, yellow cheat-line outlined in black. IRIS III was operated by the Central Signals Establishment, RAF Signals Command. IRIS is the initial letters of International Radio Installations and Systems. See photographs on page 69 and 76.

C.3

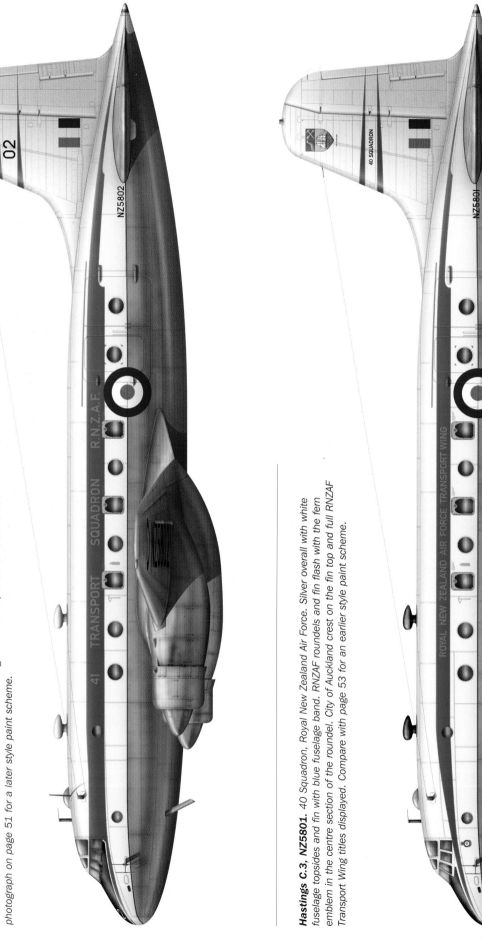

Hastings **C.3 NZ5802.** *41 Squadron, Royal New Zealand Air Force. Silver overall with white fuselage topsides, fin and rudder with blue fuselage band. RNZAF roundels and fin flash with a fern emblem in the centre section of the roundel. Last two digits of serial repeated on the fin. See photograph on page 51 for a later style paint scheme.*

Hastings **C.3, NZ5801.** *40 Squadron, Royal New Zealand Air Force. Silver overall with white fuselage topsides and fin with blue fuselage band. RNZAF roundels and fin flash with the fern emblem in the centre section of the roundel. City of Auckland crest on the fin top and full RNZAF Transport Wing titles displayed. Compare with page 53 for an earlier style paint scheme.*

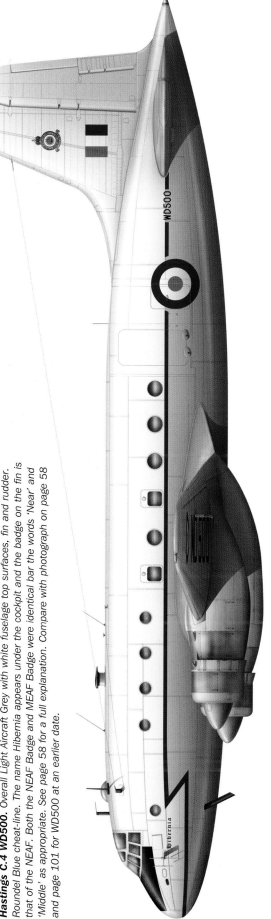

C.4

Hastings C.4 WD500. *Overall Light Aircraft Grey with white fuselage top surfaces, fin and rudder. Roundel Blue cheat-line. The name Hibernia appears under the cockpit and the badge on the fin is that of the NEAF. Both the NEAF Badge and MEAF Badge were identical bar the words 'Near' and 'Middle' as appropriate. See page 58 for a full explanation. Compare with photograph on page 58 and page 101 for WD500 at an earlier date.*

T.5

Hastings T.5 TG521. *Bomber Command Bombing School, September 1961. Silver overall with standard yellow training bands. See photograph on page 56. Also pages 57 and 66 for a later paint scheme.*

Hastings T.5 TG518. *Bomber Command Bombing School, September 1962, silver overall, with orange Day-Glo replacing the earlier yellow training bands. Type D roundels, fin flash. serials in black. See photograph on page 67.*

Hastings C.2 WD480, RAE Farnborough, February 1969. *Light Aircraft Grey overall with white fuselage topsides, fin and rudder. Dark blue cheat-line, spinner caps and engine nacelles, the latter were at a later stage repainted black. The pannier was fitted for a series of sonobuoy, radar and avionics trials. See series of photographs on page 79. Shown to advantage is the larger tailplane of the C.2 in comparison with the basic C.1.*

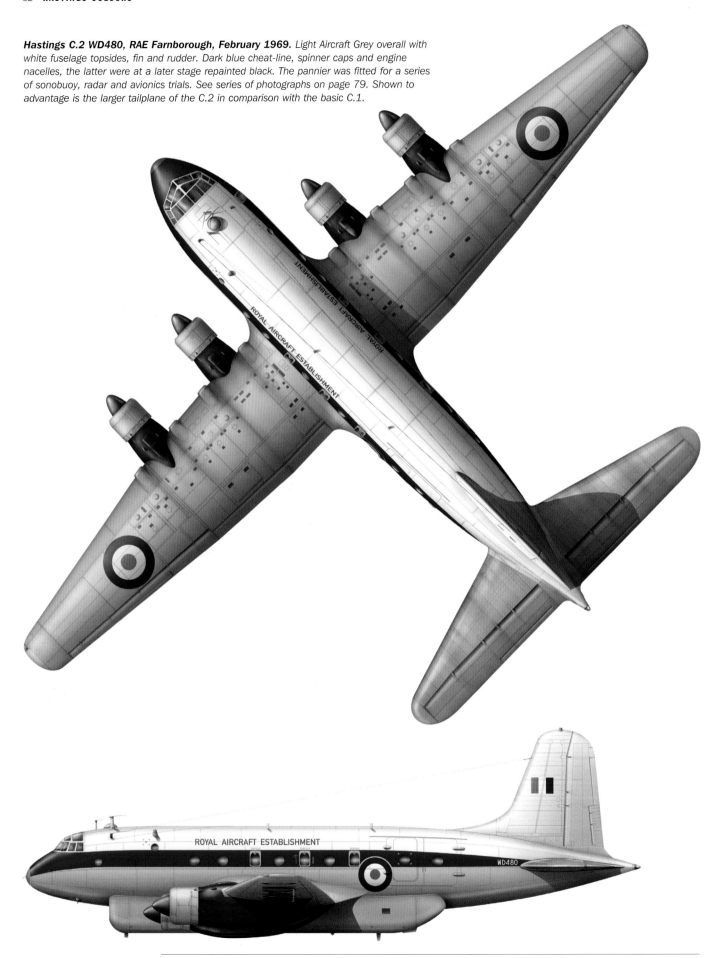

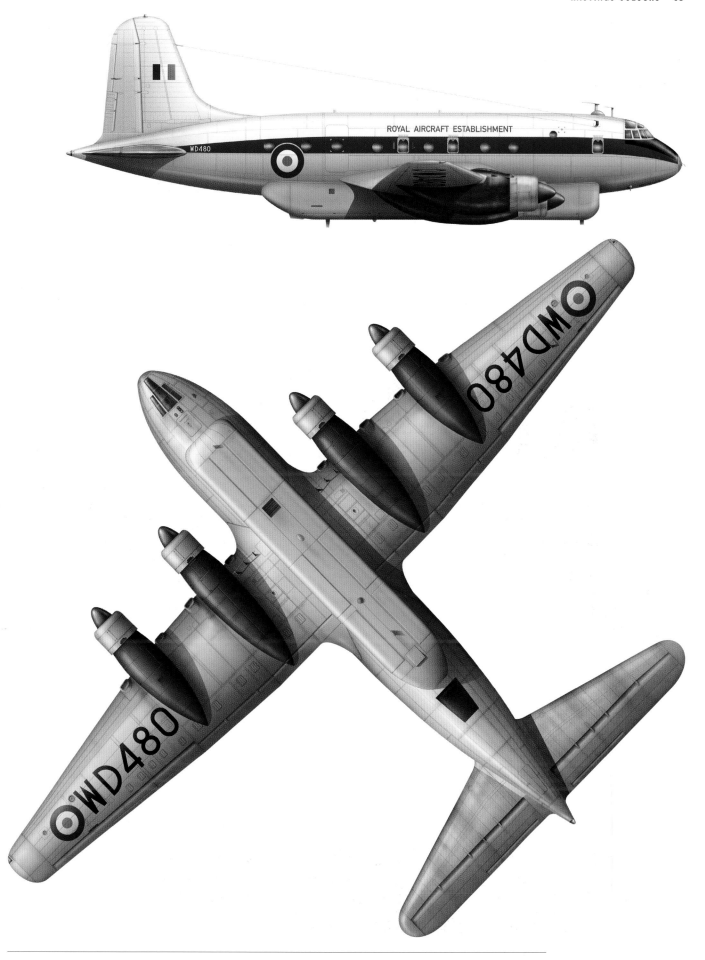

ROYAL AIRCRAFT ESTABLISHMENT

WD480

Hastings MET.1 TG622, 202 Squadron, Coastal Command. *Originally ordered as a C.1, this aircraft was one of several converted to the meteorological reconnaissance role. It was originally finished in this early camouflage scheme consisting of Medium Sea Grey upper surfaces with white undersides. The codes C - A are believed to be Extra Dark Sea Grey with the serial in black. A photograph of this aircraft appears on page 31.*

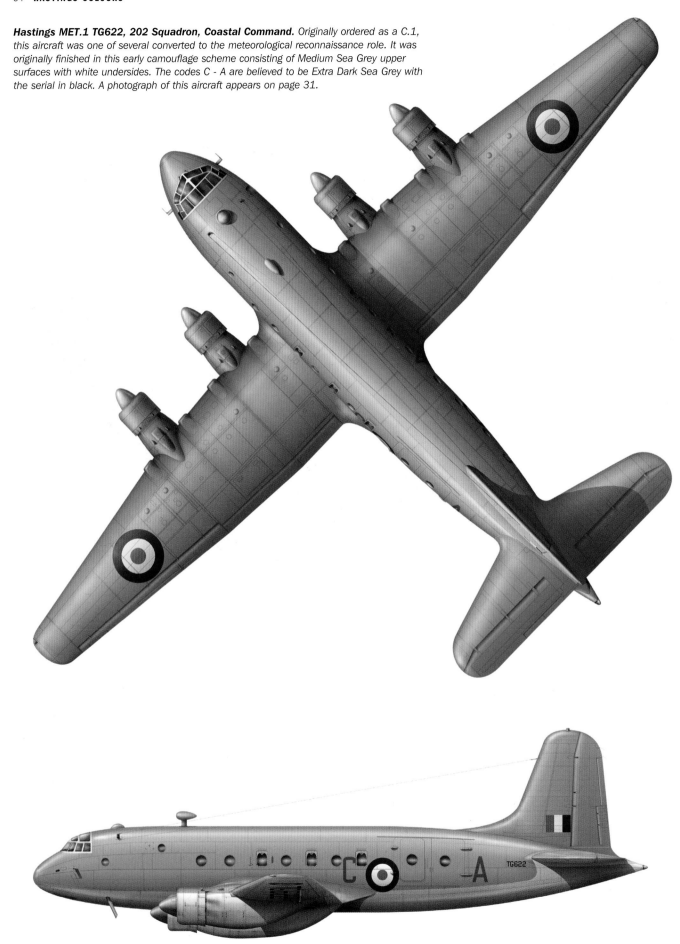

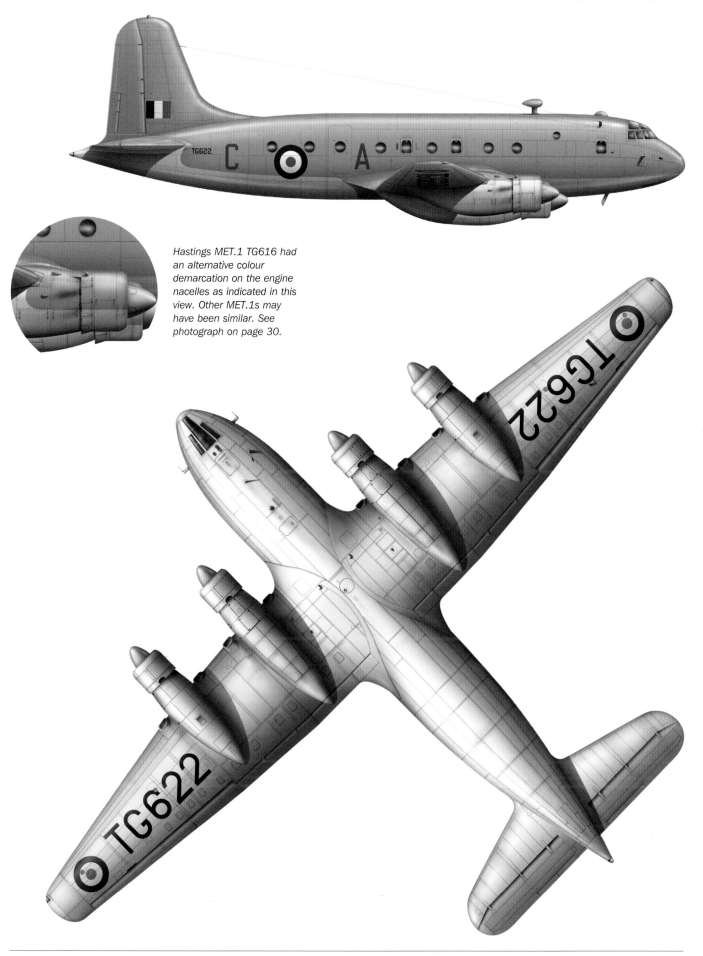

Hastings MET.1 TG616 *had an alternative colour demarcation on the engine nacelles as indicated in this view. Other MET.1s may have been similar. See photograph on page 30.*

Hastings C.1 TG621, 70 Squadron, piloted by the CO Sqn Ldr W K Greer AFC.
This aircraft was involved in the dropping of members of the 3rd Parachute Battalion at El Gamil on 5th November 1956. The jump height was approximately 600 feet and consequently all of the aircraft involved in the drop were well within small arms range. TG621 received a .303 bullet in No.1 engine, bullet damage to the tail-spar and shrapnel damage to the underside of the port mainplane.

Appendix I: **TECHNICAL DATA**

TRANSPORT

Hastings C.1

First Flight: 25th April 1947

Wing Span
Projected: 112ft 9in
Along Dihedral plane: 113ft
Wing Area: 1,408 sq ft

Wing Chord
At Root: 16ft 0.32in
At tip attachment: 6ft 11in
At extended tip: 5ft 9.81in

Wing Section Root to intermediate
Wing Outer joint: NACA 23021
   (thickness/chord ratio 21%)
Wing Extended Tip: NACA 23007
   (thickness/chord ratio 7%)

Fuselage length
Tail up: 82ft 1in
Tail Down: 80ft 9in
Diameter: 11ft
Overall Height: 22ft 5in tail down

Tailplane
Span: 43ft
Area (including elevators): 401 sq ft
Maximum Chord: 12ft
Incidence: 2° to fuselage datum line
Position: 16in above datum

Fin and Rudder
Area: 157 sq ft
Max effective chord: 14ft 4in

Control movements
Elevator: + 25°/- 17°
Aileron: + 29°/-16°
Rudder: +25°/- 25°

Flaps
Take-Off: 25% (variable)
Max Lift: 40°
Full Down: 80°

Undercarriage
Track: 24ft 8in
Main wheel tyre: Dunlop AH8291 or 50519
   64 x 22.5 x 26in
Tail wheel tyre: Dunlop AH8291 9.25 x 13in

Engine: Bristol Hercules 101 series

Fuel Capacity: 2,563 Imperial Gallons

Hydraulics
(Electro-Hydraulics) Limit 2,800 psi, Cut out
   2,450 psi

Pneumatics
(Hymatic) 600 psi

Max Take-off weight: 78,000lb

Max Landing weight: 74,000lb

Max Speed at height: 354mph at 23,700ft

Service Ceiling: 26,700ft

Production: 100

Hastings C.1A

Aircraft were converted from C.1

Wing Span
Projected: 112ft 9in
Along Dihedral plane: 113ft
Wing Area: 1,408 sq ft

Wing Chord
At Root: 16ft 0.32in
At tip attachment: 6ft 11in
At extended tip: 5ft 9.81in

Wing Section Root to intermediate
Wing Outer joint: NACA 23021
   (thickness/chord ratio 21%)
Wing Extended Tip: NACA 23007
   (thickness/chord ratio 7%)

Fuselage Length
Tail up: 82ft 1in
Tail Down: 80ft 9in
Diameter: 11ft
Overall Height: 22ft 5in tail down

Tailplane
Span: 43ft
Area (including elevators): 401 sq ft
Maximum Chord: 12ft
Incidence: 2° to fuselage datum line
Position: 16in above datum

Fin and Rudder
Area: 157 sq ft
Max effective chord: 14ft 4 in

Control movements
Elevator: + 25°/- 17°
Aileron: + 29°/-16°
Rudder: +25°/- 25°

Flaps
Take-Off: 25% (variable)
Max Lift: 40°
Full Down: 80°

Undercarriage
Track: 24ft 8in
Main wheel tyre: Dunlop AH8291 or 50519
   64 x 22.5 x 26in
Tail wheel tyre: Dunlop AH8291 9.25 x 13in

Engine: Bristol Hercules 216 series

Fuel Capacity: 2,563 Imperial Gallons +
   2 x 350 Imperial Gallon wing tanks

Hydraulics
(Electro-Hydraulics) Limit 2,800psi, Cut out
   2,450psi

Pneumatics
(Hymatic) 600psi

Max Take-Off weight: 78,000lb

Max Landing weight: 74,000lb

Max Speed at height: 354mph at 23,700ft

Service Ceiling: 26,700ft

Hastings C.2

First Flight: 14th November 1950

Wing Span
Projected: 112ft 9in
Along Dihedral plane: 113ft
Wing Area: 1,408 sq ft

Wing Chord
At Root: 16ft 0.32in
At tip attachment: 6ft 11in
At extended tip: 5ft 9.81in

Wing Section Root to intermediate
Wing Outer joint: NACA 23021
   (thickness/chord ratio 21%)
Wing Extended Tip: NACA 23007
   (thickness/chord ratio 7%)

Fuselage Length
Tail up: 82ft 1in
Tail Down: 80ft 9in
Diameter: 11ft
Overall Height: 22ft 5in tail down

Tailplane
Span: 51ft
Area (including elevators): 442 sq ft
Maximum Chord: 12ft
Incidence: 2° to fuselage datum line
Position: 16in on datum

Fin and Rudder
Area: 157 sq ft
Max effective chord: 14ft 4in

Control movements
Elevator: + 25°/- 15°
Aileron: + 29°/-16°
Rudder: +25°/- 25°

Flaps
Take-Off: 25% (variable)
Max Lift: 40°
Full Down: 80°

Undercarriage
Track: 24ft 8in
Main wheel tyre: Dunlop AH8291 or 50519
   64 x 22.5 x 26in
Tail wheel tyre: Dunlop AH8291
   9.25 x 13in

Engine: Bristol Hercules 106 & 216 series

Fuel Capacity: 3,175 Imperial Gallons

Hydraulics
(Electro-Hydraulics) Limit 2,800 psi, Cut out
   2,450 psi

Pneumatics
(Hymatic) 600 psi

Max Take-Off weight: 83,000lb

Max Landing weight: 74,000lb

Max Speed at height: 348mph at 22,200ft

Service Ceiling: 26,500ft

Production: 42

Hastings C.3

First Flight: 2nd November 1952

Wing Span
Projected: 112ft 9in
Along Dihedral plane: 113ft
Wing Area: 1,408 sq ft

Wing Chord
At Root: 16ft 0.32in
At tip attachment: 6ft 11in
At extended tip: 5ft 9.81in

Wing Section Root to intermediate
Wing Outer joint: NACA 23021
    (thickness/chord ratio 21%)
Wing Extended Tip: NACA 23007
    (thickness/chord ratio 7%)

Fuselage Length
Tail up: 82ft 1in
Tail Down: 80ft 9in
Diameter: 11ft
Overall Height: 22ft 5in tail down

Tailplane
Span: 51ft
Area (including elevators): 442 sq ft
Maximum Chord: 12ft
Incidence: 2° to fuselage datum line
Position: 16 in on datum

Fin and Rudder
Area: 157 sq ft
Max effective chord: 14ft 4in

Control movement
Elevator: + 25°/- 15°
Aileron: + 29°/-16°
Rudder: +25°/- 25°

Flaps
Take-Off: 25% (variable)
Max Lift: 40°
Full Down: 80°

Undercarriage
Track: 24ft 8in
Main wheel tyre: Dunlop AH8291 or 50519
    64 x 22.5 x 26in
Tail wheel tyre: Dunlop AH8291 9.25 x 13in

Engine: Bristol Hercules 737 series

Fuel Capacity: 3,175 Imperial Gallons

Hydraulics
(Electro-Hydraulics) Limit 2,800 psi, Cut out
    2,450 psi

Pneumatics
(Hymatic) 600 psi

Max Take-Off weight: 83,000lb

Max Landing weight: 74,000lb

Max Speed at height: 348mph at 22,200ft

Service Ceiling: 26,500ft

Production: 4

VIP TRANSPORT

Hastings C.4

First Flight: 22nd September 1951

Wing Span
Projected: 112ft 9in
Along Dihedral plane: 113 ft
Wing Area: 1,408 sq ft

Wing Chord
At Root: 16ft 0.32in
At tip attachment: 6ft 11in
At extended tip: 5ft 9.81in

Wing Section Root to intermediate
Wing Outer joint: NACA 23021
    (thickness/chord ratio 21%)
Wing Extended Tip: NACA 23007
    (thickness/chord ratio 7%)

Fuselage Length
Tail up: 82ft 1in
Tail Down: 80ft 9in
Diameter: 11ft
Overall Height: 22ft 5in tail down

Tailplane
Span: 51ft
Area (including elevators): 442 sq ft
Maximum Chord: 12ft
Incidence: 2° to fuselage datum line
Position: 16 in on datum

Fin and Rudder
Area: 157 sq ft
Max effective chord: 14ft 4in

Control movements
Elevator: + 25°/- 15°
Aileron: + 29°/-16°
Rudder: +25°/- 25°

Flaps
Take-Off: 25% (variable)
Max Lift: 40°
Full Down: 80°

Undercarriage
Track: 24ft 8in
Main wheel tyre: Dunlop AH8291 or 50519
    64 x 22.5 x 26 in
Tail wheel tyre: Dunlop AH8291
    9.25 x 13 in

Engine: Bristol Hercules 106 & 216 series

Fuel Capacity: 3,175 Imperial Gallons

Hydraulics
(Electro-Hydraulics) Limit 2,800 psi, Cut out
    2,450 psi

Pneumatics
(Hymatic) 600 psi

Max Take-Off weight: 83,000lb

Max Landing weight: 74,000lb

Max Speed at height: 348mph at 22,200ft

Service Ceiling: 26,500ft

Production: 4

METEOROLOGICAL RECONNAISSANCE

Hastings MET.1

First Flight: 27th September 1950

Wing Span
Projected: 112ft 9in
Along Dihedral plane: 113ft
Wing Area: 1,408 sq ft

Wing Chord
At Root: 16ft 0.32in
At tip attachment: 6ft 11in
At extended tip: 5ft 9.81in

Wing Section Root to intermediate
Wing Outer joint: NACA 23021
    (thickness/chord ratio 21%)
Wing Extended Tip: NACA 23007
    (thickness/chord ratio 7%)

Fuselage Length
Tail up: 82ft 1in
Tail Down: 80ft 9in
Diameter: 11ft
Overall Height: 22ft 5in tail down

Tailplane
Span: 43ft
Area (including elevators): 401 sq ft
Maximum Chord: 12ft
Incidence: 2° to fuselage datum line
Position: 16 in above datum

Fin and Rudder
Area: 157 sq ft
Max effective chord: 14ft 4in

Control movements
Elevator: + 25°/- 17°
Aileron: + 29°/-16°
Rudder: +25°/- 25°

Flaps
Take-Off: 25% (variable)
Max Lift: 40°
Full Down: 80°

Undercarriage
Track: 24 ft 8 in
Main wheel tyre: Dunlop AH8291 or 50519
    64 x 22.5 x 26 in
Tail wheel tyre: Dunlop AH8291
    9.25 x 13 in

Engine: Bristol Hercules 101 series

Fuel Capacity: 2,563 Imperial Gallons

Hydraulics
(Electro-Hydraulics) Limit 2,800 psi, Cut out
2,450 psi

Pneumatics
(Hymatic) 600 psi

Max Take-Off weight: 78,000lb

Max Landing weight: 74,000lb

Max Speed at height: 354mph at 23,700ft

Service Ceiling: 26,700ft

Production: 16 Conversions from C.1s

TRAINERS

Hastings T.5

First Flight: 1st production conversion delivered in January 1960

Wing Span
Projected: 112ft 9in
Along Dihedral plane: 113ft
Wing Area: 1,408 sq ft

Wing Chord
At Root: 16ft 0.32in
At tip attachment: 6ft 11in
At extended tip: 5ft 9.81in

Wing Section Root to intermediate
Wing Outer joint: NACA 23021
   (thickness/chord ratio 21%)
Wing Extended Tip: NACA 23007
   (thickness/chord ratio 7%)

Fuselage Length
Tail up: 82ft 1in
Tail Down: 80ft 9in
Diameter: 11ft
Overall Height: 22ft 5in tail down

Tailplane
Span: 43ft
Area (including elevators): 401 sq ft
Maximum Chord: 12ft
Incidence: 2° to fuselage datum line
Position: 16 in above datum

Fin and Rudder
Area: 157 sq ft
Max effective chord: 14ft 4in

Control movements
Elevator: + 25°/- 17°
Aileron: + 29°/-16°
Rudder: +25°/- 25°

Flaps
Take-Off: 25% (variable)
Max Lift: 40°
Full Down: 80°

Undercarriage
Track: 24ft 8in
Main wheel tyre: Dunlop AH8291 or 50519
   64 x 22.5 x 26in
Tail wheel tyre: Dunlop AH8291
   9.25 x 13in

Engine: Bristol Hercules 216 series

Fuel Capacity: 2,563 Imperial Gallons

Hydraulics
(Electro-Hydraulics) Limit 2,800 psi, Cut out
   2,450 psi

Pneumatics
(Hymatic) 600 psi

Max Take-Off weight: 78,000lb

Max Landing weight: 74,000lb

Max Speed at height: 354mph at 23,700ft

Service Ceiling: 26,700ft

Production: 8 Conversions from C.1/MET.1s

PROJECTED HASTINGS VARIANTS

There were three other versions of the Hastings that never made it into production these were as follows:

HP.73 Hastings Series II
Stretched version of C.1 with 80in forward of wing and 50in aft of wing, with an underbelly loading hatch, development ceased in 1946.

Hastings III
Basic C.1 but with rear loading doors, a mock-up of the rear fuselage was built but the aircraft was cancelled in March 1951.

HP.89 Hastings VI
Tricycle undercarriage version, with twin-bogie main undercarriage, increased wing area and rear loading doors. It was planned to use four Bristol Centaurus engines. Development stopped March 1949.

HERMES I/II/IV/V

The first two Hermes Is were identical to the Prototype Hastings and apart from the changes in the later series Hermes, i.e. stretched fuselage and tricycle undercarriage, the performance remained broadly the same. The main exception being the switch to the Bristol Proteus engine for the Hermes V.

Bristol Hercules Engine data
The Bristol Hercules engine that powered the Hastings was a 14 cylinder air-cooled 2 row-radial with sleeve valves. The four versions used on the Hastings were the series 101, and 106 which were fitted to all Mk.1 and some of the first production C.2s. The remaining C.2s and the C.4s were fitted with the Series 216 while earlier aircraft that underwent refurbishment were eventually refitted with the 216 engines also. The RNZAF Hastings C.3s were fitted from the outset with the improved Hercules 737, which was more powerful at lower altitudes, giving 2,040bhp at take-off rating. This allowed a better take-off performance and slightly higher cruising speed at altitudes below 10,000 ft. This was an improvement over the 1,640bhp in the series 101, and 1,675bhp in the 106. The improved series 216 was slightly better at 1,800bhp. All the Hastings were fitted with De Haviland hydromatic four blade propellers with a diameter of 13ft.

Opposite top: Hastings C.2 WD496 at an unknown location abroad prior to gaining a nose probe. See photograph on page 80. Tony Eastwood Collection

Opposite centre: The VIP Hastings C.4s were regular visitors to Northolt, Middlesex. WD500 is devoid of titling although it had gained the name Hibernia next to the cockpit when seen in March 1962. The Middle (or Near?) East Air Force Badge is visible on the fin. WD500's colour scheme makes an interesting comparison to that seen on page 78. Tony Eastwood Collection

Opposite bottom: Hastings C.1A TG605 of No.24 Squadron at RAF Finningley, Yorkshire in September 1967 where it was later struck off charge and received maintenance serial 7987M. Newark Air Museum

Appendix II: **HASTINGS SQUADRONS AND UNITS**

ROYAL AIR FORCE

No.24 SQUADRON

Re-equipped with Hastings: December 1950.
UK Bases: RAF Lyneham, December 1950 and moved to RAF Topcliffe, 9th February 1951. Moved to RAF Abingdon May 1953. Finally to RAF Colerne 1st January 1957.
Foreign Bases: None.
Re-equipped: January 1968 with Lockheed C-130K Hercules C.1.
Variants used: C.1/1A/2/4.

No.36 SQUADRON

Equipped with Hastings: Reformed from No.511 Squadron on 1st September 1958.
UK Bases: RAF Colerne.
Foreign Bases: None.
Re-equipped: From late July 1967 with Hercules C.1.
Variants used: C.1/1A/C.2.

No.47 SQUADRON

Re-equipped with Hastings: September 1948.
UK Bases: RAF Dishforth September 1948, moved to Schleswigland November 1948. RAF Topcliffe 22nd August 1949, RAF Abingdon May 1953.
Foreign Bases: Schleswigland, West Germany for *Operation Plainfare*.
Re-equipped: From March 1956 converted to Blackburn Beverley C.1.
Variants used: C.1/1A/C.2.

No.48 SQUADRON

Re-equipped with Hastings: Mid-1957.
UK Bases: None.
Foreign Bases: RAF Changi, Singapore.
Disbanded: March 1967.
Variants used: C.1/1A/C.2.

No.51 SQUADRON

Equipped with Hastings: Utilised two Hastings from 1963 to 1968.
UK Bases: RAF Watton.
Foreign Bases: None.
Variants used: C.1/C.1A.

No.53 SQUADRON

Equipped with Hastings: 1st August 1949.
UK Bases: Reformed RAF Topcliffe 1st August 1949, moved to RAF Lyneham 9th February 1951.
Foreign Bases: Detached to Schleswigland then Wunsdorf, West Germany, October 1949, re Berlin Airlift duties.
Re-equipped: From February 1957 converted to Blackburn Beverley. Relinquished Hastings December 1956.
Variants used: C.1.

No.70 SQUADRON

Re-equipped with Hastings: December 1955.
UK Bases: None.
Foreign Bases: Nicosia, Cyprus, 1955, Akrotiri July 1966.
Re-equipped: November 1967 converted to Armstrong Whitworth Argosy. However one Hastings retained for VIP duties until July 1968.
Variants used: C.1/1A/2/4.

No.99 SQUADRON

Re-equipped with Hastings: August 1949, initial cadre of crews commenced training while Squadron was involved in *Operation Plainfare* with Avro Yorks.
UK Bases: RAF Lyneham.
Foreign Bases: None.
Re-equipped: June 1959 converted to Bristol Britannia.
Variants used: C.1/1A/C.2.

No.114 SQUADRON

Re-equipped with Hastings: 5th May 1959.
UK Bases: RAF Colerne.
Foreign Bases: None.
Disbanded: 30th September 1961. (Reformed following day at Benson as the first recipient of the Armstrong Whitworth Argosy, received from February 1962).
Variants used: C.1/1A/C.2.

No.202 SQUADRON

Re-equipped with Hastings: Late 1950 and assigned to Coastal Command.
UK Bases: RAF Aldergrove.
Foreign Bases: None.
Disbanded: 31 July 1964.
Variants used: MET.1

No.242 SQUADRON

Re-equipped with Hastings: August 1949.
UK Bases: RAF Lyneham.
Foreign Bases: None.
Disbanded: 1st May 1950.
Variants used: C.1

No.297 SQUADRON

Re-equipped with Hastings: 17th October 1948.
UK Bases: RAF Dishforth October 1948, moved to Germany for *Operation Plainfare*. Returned to RAF Topcliffe 13th December 1949.
Foreign Bases: Schleswigland 13th December 1948 to 1949.
Disbanded: 15 November 1950.
Variants used: C.1

No.511 SQUADRON

Re-equipped with Hastings: September 1949.
UK Bases: RAF Lyneham from September 1949, moved to RAF Colerne 1957. No.511 Squadron disbanded to become No.36 Squadron on 1st September 1958.
Foreign Bases: None.
Disbanded: 1st September 1958.
Variants used: C.1/1A/C.2.

NO.230 OPERATIONAL CONVERSION UNIT

Received Hastings: 1st January (or 1st July) 1974 (sources conflict): relinquished Hastings July 1977.
UK Base: RAF Scampton. Known as the Hastings Radar Flight used to train Vulcan crews on radar. Whilst attached to No.230 OCU the Flight acquired the unofficial designation '1066 Squadron'.
Foreign Bases: None.
Variants used: T.5.

NO.241 OPERATIONAL CONVERSION UNIT

Received Hastings: January 1950.
UK Bases: RAF Dishforth January 1950.
Foreign Bases: None.
Disbanded: Merged with No.240 OCU (from North Luffenham) to form No.242 OCU, 16th April 1951.
Variants used: C.1.

NO.242 OPERATIONAL CONVERSION UNIT

Received Hastings: 16th April 1951 upon merger of No.240 and No.241 OCU.
UK Bases: RAF Dishforth, moved to RAF Thorney Island, February 1962.
Foreign Bases: None
Disbanded: March 1967
Variants used: C.1/C.1A

OTHER HASTINGS UNITS

CENTRAL SIGNALS ESTABLISHMENT (CSE)

Re-equipped with Hastings: Nos. 97, 115, 116 and 151 Squadron and various units within Signals Command used Hastings; the best known being IRIS II & III.
UK Bases: RAF Watton.
Foreign Bases: None.
Variants used: C.1/C.2.

BOMBER COMMAND BOMBING SCHOOL (BCBS)

Re-equipped with Hastings: From 1959
UK Base: RAF Lindholme
Foreign Bases: None
Disbanded: With the merger of individual Commands into Strike Command, the unit was retitled Strike Command Bombing School on 30th April 1968.
Variant used: T.5.

STRIKE COMMAND BOMBING SCHOOL (SCBS)

UK Bases: RAF Lindholme 30th April 1968. Moved to RAF Scampton 1st September 1972 until disbanded 1st January (or 1st July) 1974 (sources conflict). A Hastings flight was merged with No.230 OCU (*q.v.*) in 1974, becoming the Hasting's Radar Flight.
Variants used: C.1A/T.5.

No.1 PARACHUTE TRAINING SCHOOL

UK Bases: RAF Abingdon.
Foreign Bases: None.
Variants used: C.1.

TRANSPORT COMMAND DEVELOPMENT UNIT/FLIGHT

UK Base: RAF Abingdon. 1st July 1949.
Disbanded: 1st February 1957.
Variants used: C.1, C.2.

TRANSPORT COMMAND AIRBORNE SUPPORT FLIGHT

Re-numbered No.1312 Flight on 14th September 1954.

No.1312 (TRANSPORT SUPPORT) FLIGHT

Formed: 14th September 1954.
Disbanded: 1st April 1957.
UK Base: RAF Abingdon.
Variants used: C.1/C.2

RAF FLYING COLLEGE

UK Base: RAF Manby
Variants used: C.1/C.2

MIDDLE EAST COMMAND COMMUNICATION SQUADRON

Reformed: 1st October 1961.
Foreign Base: RAF Khormaksar, Aden
Disbanded: 1st September 1967, having been reduced to a Flight by 15th June 1965.
Variants used: C.4 (Hastings used within above dates but not necessarily to the end of the unit's existance).

FAR EAST COMMUNICATION SQUADRON

Formed: Assumed this title on 25th May 1949 from earlier Flight status moving to RAF Tengah 21st August 1949 before returning to RAF Changi.
Foreign Base: Changi, Singapore from 1st January 1952.
Disbanded: 17th February 1959.
Variants used: C.1/C.2/C.4

AEROPLANE & ARMAMENT EXPERIMENTAL ESTABLISHMENT

Base: Boscombe Down
Used various Hastings for trials.

AIRBORNE FORCES EXPERIMENTAL ESTABLISHMENT

Used Hastings from April 1947, until trials completed.
Base: Beaulieu.

RADAR RECONNAISSANCE FLIGHT

Base: RAF Wyton.

ROYAL AIRCRAFT ESTABLISHMENT

Base: Farnborough.
Variants used: C.1/C.1A/C.2.

METEOROLOGICAL RESEARCH FLIGHT

Base: Farnborough from 1953 until retirement.

ROYAL NEW ZEALAND AIR FORCE

No.40 Squadron
Re-equipped with Hastings: Re-numbered from No.41 Squadron December 1954.
Base: Whenuapai.
Disbanded: 1966.
Variant used: C.3.

No.41 Squadron
Re-equipped with Hastings: Nov. 1952.
Base: Whenuapai.
Disbanded: Re-numbered No.40 Squadron.
Variant used: C.3.

IN ADDITION:

EMPIRE FLYING SCHOOL
Disbanded into RAFFC. 31st July 1949. Used Hastings TG507.

TRANSPORT COMMAND EXAMINING UNIT
Later became Air Support Command Examining Unit 1st August 1967. Used at least one Hastings during the unit's history.

TRANSPORT COMMAND TRAINING AND DEVELOPMENT FLIGHT
Formed 14th October 1951 at RAF Abingdon. Disbanded 1st February 1957 at RAF Benson. Used several Hastings C.1/C.2 including TG582.

Below: Hastings C.1 TG537 of No.242 Squadron, visiting RAF Horsham St Faith in 1950. This is a very rare image of a 242 Squadron Hastings, which only operated the type from August 1949 to 1st May 1950. Its existence as a Hastings unit is often overlooked, presumably because of the later existence of No.242 OCU. B A Forward via P H T Green

Appendix III: **HASTINGS AND HERMES PRODUCTION**

HP67 HASTINGS

Prototypes

TE580 AFEE, A&AEE, SOC to CAA Fire School Stansted

TE583 A&AEE, AFEE, HP, RRE, SOC 7/4/65 to CTE Manston

PRODUCTION HASTINGS C.1

Hastings C.1s were ordered under contract 6/AFCT/4186/CB.6(a) and allocated serial numbers TG499 to TG537, TG551 to TG587, and finally TG601 to TG624.

Note: Regarding aircraft shown as struck of charge (SOC), in some instances the aircraft were delivered to their final destination and then declared SOC days later, or in some cases up to a month after the delivery flight.

Bold entries denote airframe extant as at May 2008.

TG499 A&AEE, AFEE, crashed at Beacon Hill, Wilts on 26/9/49.

TG500 A&AEE, AFEE, A&AEE, SOC Boscombe Down 12/4/73 to 71MU RAF Bicester for GI use.

TG501 HP, A&AEE, ETPS RAE Farnborough, SOC to CTE Manston 29/3/66.

TG502 RAE, A&AEE, RAE, A&AEE, AFEE, SOC Boscombe Down 15/12/72 to St Mawgan for FCRT, finally expiring late 1977.

TG503 A&AEE, AFEE, WIE, RRE Radar Research Flt, con to T.5, BCBS SCBS 230 OCU, to Gatow 6/77 moved to the Alliierten Museum 9/97 currently on display.

TG504 A&AEE, 47, con to MET.1, 202 SOC 8/8/66 to Finningley for FCRT.

TG505 47, con to MET.1 202, con to T.5, A&AEE, BCBS, SCBS, 230 OCU, to St Athan 1977 dismantled and moved by road to Hereford for the SAS, last seen departing on lorry 5/82 for scrap.

TG506 PTU, WEE, RAE, WEE PTU, A&AEE, 24/36 202, SOC to CTE Manston 29/3/66.

TG507 EFS, 47, 202, 24/36, 242 OCU HP, 51, SOC 31/10/68.

TG508 EFS, 47, 202, 53/99, 242 OCU crashed at Thorney Island 7/3/62.

TG509 A&AEE, RRE, 53/99/511, 242 OCU, 70, SOC 9/11/67 at Akrotiri.

TG510 47, 242OCU, 24, 47, 1312Flt, 511, 36, 242 OCU SOC 1.11.66 to Cambridge Airport for FCRT, finally expired 11/84.

TG511 47, 99/511, 202, con to T.5 BCBS, SCBS. Made last RAF Hastings flight when it was delivered to Cosford 8/77. Now preserved within the National Cold War Museum.

TG512 TCDU, 241 OCU, 53/99/511, SOC 27/11/59 to Tangmere.

TG513 53/99, 511, 242 OCU, 70, 24/36 SOC 8/9/67 to CTE Manston.

TG514 47, HP for VIP mock up use, con to MET.1 202, RRE SOC at Pershore 1967.

TG515 TCDU, 53/99, 242 OCU, SOC 4/11/59.

TG516 53/99/511, 99, 36, 48, SOC 21/1/72.

TG517 47, 53, con to MET.1 202, con to T.5 BCBS, SCBS 230 OCU to Winthorpe airfield 6/77 current at Newark Air Museum.

TG518 47, con to MET.1, 202, con to T.5 BCBS, SCBS, SOC 13/5/69 to Carlisle for FCRT.

TG519 47, crashed at Dishforth 2/10/48 became GIA 6609M subsequently scrapped.

TG520 47, 24/47, 48, FECS, 48, FECS 48, SOC 27/2/67 to Gan for FCRT.

TG521 47, CA, 53/99, 53, 242 OCU, con to T.5, BCBS, SCBS SOC 9/7/71.

TG522 47, 53/99, 36, crashed at Khartoum 29/5/59.

TG523 47, 53/99, 47, 24, 70, 48, SOC 15/2/67.

TG524 47, 53/99/511, 114, A&AEE, 70, 24/36, 70, SOC 2/7/71.

TG525 47, 53/99, 48, SOC 9/3/67 to Paya Lebar for FCRT.

TG526 47, 242, 24, 24/47, 70, 48, SOC 9/3/67.

TG527 47, 24/47 CA, 24, 24/36/114, 24, A&AEE, BCBS, SCBS, SOC 4/11/68 at Abingdon.

TG528 47, 53/99, 242 OCU, 24/36, 24 SOC 25/1/68 Sold to Skyfame collection, transferred to IWM Duxford 1979, current.

TG529 47, 53/99, con to T.5, BCBS, SCBS SOC 30/4/69 to CAA Fire School Stansted.

TG530 47, 53/99, 242 OCU, 70, 151, 51, SOC 29/8/67 to Lindholme.

TG531 53/99/511, 48, SOC 1/11/66.

TG532 53/99, 24, 36, 24/36, SOC 14/1/66 to Lindholme.

TG533 A&AEE, AFEE, MET.1 mock up, 202, 242 OCU, 24/36, 70, SOC 18/12/67 to Bassingbourn for FCRT.

TG534 47, Destroyed by fire at Schleswigland 6/4/49.

TG535 241 OCU, 242 OCU, 70, 224/36 70, SOC 13/1/68 to Odiham for FCRT.

TG536 241 OCU, 47, 47/53, 53/99/511, 242 OCU, 48, 242 OCU, BCBS, SCBS, SOC 1974, to Colerne Museum then to FF&SS Catterick early 1976. Parts used in Halifax recreation at the Yorkshire Air Museum, Elvington.

TG537 24, 511, 36, 242, 24/36, 242 OCU, SOC 8/8/66.

TG551 53/99, 242 OCU, 70, 24/36, 70, SOC 5/11/67 to Far East.

TG552 Crashed at Negombo, Ceylon (Sri Lanka) 12/4/51.

TG553 47, 99/511, con to T.5, BCBS, SCBS, SOC /74 to Fairford for FCRT.

TG554 202, 242 OCU, 53/99, 242 OCU, SOC 4/11/59.

TG555 241 OCU, 242 OCU, SOC 6/2/60.

TG556 53/99/511, 24, 24/36, SOC 25/8/67 to Watton for FCRT.

TG557 53/99/511, 511, 36, 114, 70, 24/36 SOC 3/9/68.

TG558 24/47, SOC 4/11/59.

TG559 24/47, crashed at Abingdon 9/10/53, became GIA 7108M.

TG560 CSE, 116, Named IRIS II, SOC 4/3/58.

TG561 242 OCU, 70, SOC 8/2/67 to Nicosia for FCRT.

TG562 242 OCU, crashed on take-off at Topcliffe 14/3/52.

TG563 241 OCU, 47, 53/99, 242 OCU, 99, 70, SOC 31/10/67 to Northolt for FCRT, finally expiring during 1977.

TG564 53/99, undershot and crashed at Kai Tak 27/7/53.

TG565 Lyneham con to MET.1, 202, 242 OCU, A&AEE 202, SOC 30/11/66 to FF&SS Catterick.

TG566 241 OCU, con to MET.1, 242 OCU, 202, crashed on take-off at Aldergrove 19/9/62.

TG567 241 OCU, con to MET.1, 202, A&AEE, SOC 1/6/66.

TG568 TCDU, PTS, A&AEE, SCBS, SOC 19/2/74 to Bedford for FCRT, finally expired late 1986.

TG569 242 OCU, 53/99 48, SOC 1/11/66.

TG570 241 OCU, 242 OCU, 48, 242 OCU, SOC 11/11/67 to FF&SS Catterick.

TG571 241 OCU, 24, 1312 Flt, 99, 70, 24/36, 242 OCU, SOC 7/6/67 to Benson.

TG572 241 OCU, 242 OCU, con to MET.1 202, SOC 31/8/66 to Shawbury

TG573 241 OCU, 47, 53/99 SOC 22/1/59 to GIA as 7594M

TG574 242, 241 OCU, 99, 53, crashed at Benina, Libya 20/12/50

TG575 241 OCU, 24, 70, crashed while landing at El Adem, Libya 4/5/66

TG576 241 OCU, 202, 242 OCU, 70, 24/36 SOC 22/8/67 to Gutersloh for FCRT

TG577 241 OCU, 242 OCU, 53/99, 511, 36, 70, 24/36 crashed near Abingdon after structural failure 6/7/65

TG578 241 OCU, 53/99, 242 OCU, SOC 4/11/59

TG579 241 OCU, TCASF, 242 OCU, 48, crashed into Indian Ocean near Gan 1/3/60

TG580 241 OCU, TCASF, 24/47, 48, crash-landed at Gan 3/7/59 dumped into the Indian Ocean after spares recovery.

TG581 241 OCU, 242 OCU, 24/36, SOC 23/8/67 to CAA Fire School Stansted

TG582 241 OCU, 242 OCU, TCDF, 47, 24, 70, 24/36, SOC 30/12/65

TG583 242, 241 OCU, crashed on finals to Dishforth 31/7/50

TG584 241 OCU, 53/99, 242 OCU, crashed while overshooting at Dishforth 13/9/55

TG585 241 OCU, 242 OCU, SOC 8/2/60

TG586 241 OCU, 242 OCU, SOC 4/11/59

TG587 242 OCU, 53/99/511, 36, 242 OCU, SOC 17/8/67 to Topcliffe for FCRT

TG601 1 PTS, 24/47, 1312 Flt, 24, 47, 242 OCU, SOC 23/11/59

TG602 1 PTS, TCASF, crashed at ShalJufa 12/1/53

TG603 24, 99, w/o Luqa 16/6/52

TG604 241 OCU, 242, 53/99, 242 OCU, 24/36, SOC 15/8/67

TG605 24, 53/99, 24, 114, 24/36, SOC 7/11/67 to Finningley as 7987M

TG606 24/47, 24, 114, 70, SOC 30/11/66 to Abingdon

TG607 24, 24/36/114, SOC 1/8/67 to Wildenrath

TG608 24, 24/47, 511, 70, 242 OCU, SOC 21/9/67 to Leeming

TG609 24, 242 OCU, SOC 8/2/60

TG610 53/99, 47, 53/99, 48, 242 OCU, crash landed at Thorney Island 17/12/63

TG611 Dishforth Wing, crashed at Tegel 16/7/49

TG612 241 OCU, 242 OCU, 70, 48, SOC 14/11/66

TG613 47, 242, 53/99, ditched into Mediterranean Sea 22/7/53

TG614 24/47, TCASF, 24/47, 70, 48, SOC 9/3/67

TG615 1 PTS, TCASF, 24/47, 1312Flt, crashed near to Colerne 21/10/57

TG616 511, 53/99, 114, 36, 242 OCU, SOC 27/11/67 to Marham

TG617 RAFFC, 242 OCU, SOC 16/12/59 to Old Sarum

TG618 RAE, Met RF, SOC 29/9/68

TG619 RAE, Met RF, SOC 1/70.

TG620 Con to MET.1, 202, Con C.1, 36, 24/36, 48, SOC 9/3/67.

TG621 Con to MET.1, 202, Con C.1, 70, 202, 24/36, 24, SOC 12/2/68 to Lyneham.

TG622 Con to MET.1, 202, SOC 31/10/66 to North Coates.

TG623 Con to MET.1, 202, A&AEE, RRE, 202 SOC 3/3/67 to CTE Manston for FCRT.

TG624 Con to MET.1, 202, crashed on take-off at Aldergrove 27/12/61.

HP67 HASTINGS C.2

65 Hastings C.2s with serials allocated as follows under contract 6/ACFT/3582/CB.6(a). WD475 to WD505 and WD543 to WD576. This order was amended to just 25 Hastings C.2, the 26th (WD500) however, became the first C.4.

WD475 A&AEE, 224/47 53/99/511 511, 36, 114, 24/36, 70, SOC 6/12/67 to Wittering.

WD476 A&AEE, CA, 511, 24, 24/36, 24, SOC 25/9/69.

WD477 A&AEE, 511, 24/36, 24, SOC 30/1/68 to Lindholme.

WD478 RAFFC, crashed after take-off at RAF Strubby 19/3/51.

WD479 24/47, 24, 48, SOC 6/3/67.

WD480 RAE, SOC 25/9/74 at Farnborough for FCRT expired during 198.

WD481 511, 53/99/511, 511, 36, 114, 48, SOC 25/4/67 to Wyton.

WD482 RRE, SOC 1/5/67.

WD483 24/47, 70, crashed at Ataq 9/4/56

WD484 RRE, Crashed at Boscombe Down 2/3/55

WD485 24/47, TCASF, 1312Flt, 99, 36, 114, 24/36, 24, SOC 25/9/69

WD486 1 PTS, 24/47, 511, 24/47, 24, 114, 70, SOC 29/11/67 to Bicester

WD487 1 PTS, 24/47, TCASF, 24, 24/36, 24, SOC 14/8/68

WD488 24/47, 511, 53/99/511, 511, 36, 48, SOC 26/11/65

WD489 47, 24, 70, SOC 12/2/68

WD490 24/47, 48, 70, SOC 11/10/67 to Bicester as 7985M

WD491 24/47, 53/99/511, 24, 24/36, crashed at West Raynham 9/6/67

WD492 47, crashed onto Greenland Ice cap 16/9/52

WD493 TCDU, TCDF, 24, 24/36, SOC 2/2/68 to Scampton 1968

WD494 24, 47, RAFFC, 24/47, 24, 24/36, 24, SOC 7/2/68 to CAA Fire School Stansted

WD495 47, 1312Flt, 99, 36, 114, 24/36, 24, SOC 7/2/68

WD496 CA, A&AEE, accident at Boscombe Down 21/9/73 placed onto fire dump; finally removed as scrap during July 1989

WD497 47, TCASF, 53/99/511, 511, 36, 48, crashed at Seletar 29/5/61

WD498 24/47, TCASF, 48, A&AEE, 70, crashed at El Adem 10/10/61

WD499 RAFFC, 53/99/511, 24, 24/36, 48, RRE, SOC 30/9/74 at Pershore, moved to Honington by road for FCRT 1979, burnt by 8/85 and removed as scrap.

HASTINGS C.4

WD500 A&AEE, 24, FECS, 24,70, SOC 31/1/70

WJ324 24,70, FECS, SOC 9/3/67

WJ325 MoS, HP, FECS, 24, Khormaksar, Stn Flt, MECS, FECS, SOC 28/3/68 to Luqa

WJ326 24/47, FECS, MECS, SOC 2/7/71

HASTINGS C.2

The third order for 20 Hastings C.2s was under contract 6/AFCT/5882/CB.6(a). They were allocated serials WJ324 to WJ343, although the first three became Hastings C.4s.

WJ327 RAFFC, 24, 99, 24, 24/36, 24, RAE, SOC 29/5/73 at Farnborough.

WJ328 511, 70, 36, 70, A&AEE 70, SOC 28/3/68 to Luqa 1968.

WJ329 511, 53/99/511, 511, 36, 24/36/114, 24, SOC 25/9/69 to Leeming rear fuselage reappeared during 1982.

WJ330 RAFFC, 511, 99, 24, 114, 24/36, 24, SOC 25/9/69.

WJ331 511, 99, 24, 24/36/114, 24, SOC 15/2/71.

WJ332 511, 53/99/511, 99, 24, 114, 48, FECS, SOC 13/8/68 to Gan for FCRT.

WJ333 511, 53/99/511, 36, 48, FECS, SOC 14/3/67.

WJ334 511, 36, 24/36, 24, SOC 5/2/68 to Manby 1968.

WJ335 511, crashed at Abingdon 22/6/53.

WJ336 511, 48, SOC 5/11/68.

WJ337 511, 53/99/511, 70, 99, 24, 114, 48, FECS SOC 5/11/68

WJ338 511, CSE, CSDS, 151, 97, 115, RRE, Named IRIS III SOC 4/7/69 to Catterick

WJ339 511, 53/99/511, 99, 24, 24/36, 24, SOC 25/9/69

WJ340 511, 53/99/511, 24, 24/36, 24, SOC 7/2/68 to Strubby

WJ341 511, 24/47, crashed at Abingdon 26/7/55

WJ342 24/47, 47, 511, 36, crashed at Eastleigh, Kenya 23/1/61

WJ343 last aircraft delivered 17/10/52. 511, 99, 36, 24/36, 24, SOC 25/9/65

HP94 HASTINGS C.4

See above

EXPORTS
HP95 HASTINGS C.3

NZ5801 41, 40, last flight 2 February 1966. Scrapped at Ohakea 2/71, forward fuselage and other parts to MOTAT 18/2/71.

NZ5802 41, 40, wfu Whenuapai 5/65. flown to Ohakea for storage 2/66 scrapped 8/69.

NZ5803 41, 40, wfu Whenuapai 5/65. flown to Ohakea for storage 2/66 scrapped 8/69.

NZ5804 41, 40, w/o Darwin, Australia 9/9/55.

TOTAL HASTINGS PRODUCTION: 152

HP HERMES

HP68 HERMES I

G-AGSS: HP, written off 2/12/45.

HP74 HERMES II

G-AGUB: HP, MoS, allocated military serial VX234, to RRE Defford 10/53. Scrapped 1968.

HP81 HERMES IV

G-AKFP: BOAC Named 'Hamilcar'; Airwork, allocated military serial XD632; to Airwork, w/o 1/9/57.

G-ALDA: BOAC, Named 'Hecuba'; Airwork allocated WZ838, Falcon Airways, Air Safaris Ltd, Air Links, retired to Southend 12/64. Scrapped 1965.

G-ALDB: BOAC, Named 'Hebe' Airwork as WZ839. W/o Pithiviers France 23/7/52.

G-ALDC: BOAC, Named 'Hermione', Airwork as WZ840, Falcon Airways, Named 'James Robertson Justice' w/o Southend 9/10/60.

G-ALDD: BOAC, Named 'Horatius' Skyways, wfu and Scrapped July 1959

G-ALDE: BOAC, Named 'Hanno', Skyways, Bahamas Airways as VP-BBQ, G-ALDE Air Safaris, wfu scrapped Hurn 5/62

G-ALDF: BOAC, Named 'Hadrian' WZ841 crashed in sea of Sicily 25/8/52

G-ALDG: BOAC, Named 'Horsa', Airwork, Falcon Airways, Britavia, Silver City Named 'City of Chester' retired at Gatwick and used as training airframe, moved to Duxford during January 1981.

G-ALDH: BOAC, Named 'Heracles', Skyways w/o at Heathrow after undercarriage collapse, scrapped at Stansted.

G-ALDI: BOAC, Named 'Hannibal' Britavia, XJ309, silver City, Named 'City of Coventry' retired to Stansted 10/10/62 and scrapped.

G-ALDJ: BOAC, Named 'Hengist', Britavia, w/o while landing at Blackbushe at night 5/11/56.

G-ALDK: BOAC, Named 'Helena' Britavia, XJ281, w/o after crash landing at Drigh Road, Karachi, Pakistan 5/8/56.

G-ALDL: BOAC, Named 'Hector' Skyways, Bahamas Airways as VP-BBP, G-ALDL, Air Safaris, Skyways Air Links, to Southend 31/8/62 used as spares source for G-ALDA

G-ALDM: BOAC, Named 'Hero' Air Safaris, Silver City, Scrapped Hurn 5/68

G-ALDN: BOAC, Named 'Horus' Forced landed in Sahara desert 26/5/52 150 miles SE of Port Etienne, French West Africa, now Novahibov, Mauritannia.

G-ALDO: BOAC, Named 'Heron' Airwork, scrapped Blackbushe 3/59

G-ALDP: BOAC, Named 'Homer' Britavia, XJ269, Silver City, 'Named City of Truro' flown to Stansted for scrapping 10/10/62

G-ALDR: BOAC, Named 'Herodotus' Skyways, wfu 8/59 and scrapped at Stansted

G-ALDS: BOAC, Named 'Hesperides' Skyways, wfu 1/60 and scrapped at Stansted

G-ALDT: BOAC, Named 'Hestia' Skyways, MEA as OD-ACB, G-ALDT, Bahamas Airways as VP-BBQ, G-ALDT, Air Safaris, Skyways wfu 6/62 and scrapped at Stansted

G-ALDU: BOAC, Named 'Halcyone' Britavia, XJ280, Kuwait Airways, Silver City named 'City of Gloucester' scrapped at Stansted 1/1/62

G-ALDV: BOAC, Named 'Hera' Skyways w/o after crash at Meesden Green, Hertfordshire 1/4/58

G-ALDW: BOAC, Named 'Helios' Skyways, blown up by EOKA at Nicosia, Cyprus 4/3/56

G-ALDX: BOAC, Named 'Hyperion' Britavia, XJ276, Kuwait Airways, Wfu 1/60

G-ALDY: BOAC, Named 'Honor' Skyways, MEA as OD-ACC, G-ALDY Skyways until wfu at Stansted 12/58

HP82 HERMES V

G-ALEU HP, w/o 10/4/51 after crash landing at Chilbolton, to Boscombe Down for spares then sold to Airwork.

G-ALEV HP, dismantled at Farnborough 9/53 fuselage by road to Southend during 1958 for Aviation Traders for use in freight door conversion.

TOTAL HERMES PRODUCTION: 29

Appendix IV: HASTINGS WRITTEN-OFF IN SERVICE

A brief summary of those Hastings written-off following an accident/incident in service, listed by serial number. A location, date, brief outline of circumstances (if known) and the number of fatalities (if incurred) are included. Thirty four Hastings fall into the above category, 14 of which (denoted F) involved fatalities numbering 116 persons - including two killed on the ground.

The first Hastings to be written-off was TG519 on 2nd October 1948; the last was WD491 on 9th June 1967.

TG499
F
Wiltshire, 26th September 1949. An underslung container termed a paratechnicon became detached in flight during a trial, it pivoted back, struck the tailplane and the aircraft crashed from approximately 4000 feet. All three crew members aboard were killed.

TG508
RAF Thorney Island, 7th March 1962. Crashed while landing in a crosswind and caught fire.

TG519
RAF Dishforth, 2nd October 1948. Undershot runway during a three-engined approach; the impact severed the port undercarriage. Became 6609M.

TG522
F
Khartoum, Sudan, 29th May 1959. One engine failed following departure from Khartoum, and the aircraft returned to the airport, stalled on finals and crashed. The crew of five were killed, although all 25 passengers aboard survived; albeit injured.

TG534
Schleswigland, 6th April 1949. Whilst starting up, an engine caught fire; the ensuing blaze gutted the aircraft.

TG552
RAF Negombo, Ceylon (Sri Lanka). 12th April 1951. Crashed whilst landing, left the runway and severed its port wing. Note: sources differ by stating it crashed at Lyneham. It didn't.

TG559
RAF Abingdon, 9th October 1953. Struck the ground in poor visibility, possibly at night (sources conflict on this point). Struck off charge and became ground instruction airframe 7108M.

TG562
RAF Topcliffe, 14th March 1952. Crashed shortly after take-off. Note. Sources conflict; some state that this aircraft crashed at RAF Fayid, Egypt. Whatever the truth, this aircraft was written-off on this date.

TG564
F
Kai Tak, Hong Kong, 27th July 1953. Whilst landing, undershot the airfield striking a hut with its undercarriage, (killing an occupant) and crashed. A fire ensued, it spread and the aircraft was burnt out.

TG574
F
Benina (near Benghazi), Libya, 20th December 1950. En-route to Tripoli whilst carrying airmen home to the UK, a propeller blade became detached from the inboard port engine, entered the Hastings's fuselage severing elevator and other control lines. The engine then fell away. Benina was reached, but the aircraft was very difficult to control and on landing turned upside down crushing the flight-deck. Five persons died ; 29 (including all 27 passengers) survived.

TG575
El Adem, Libya, Egypt, 4th May 1966. Whilst landing, one of the undercarriage legs collapsed followed shortly after by the other, during which time an engine caught fire as the aircraft came to rest. The fire was soon extinguished but the Hasting was damaged beyond repair.

TG577
F
Little Baldon, Oxfordshire, 6th July 1965. This aircraft took off from RAF Abingdon carrying six crew members and 35 paratroops. Shortly after take-off the Hastings climbed toward the vertical, stalled, then fell inverted into a field, killing all 41 occupants. This was the worst casualty figure of any of the 14 fatal accidents involving the Hastings. Metal fatigue of two of the elevator bolts was suspected.

TG579
RAF Gan, Maldives, Indian Ocean, 1st March 1960. As this aircraft approached Gan to land, at night, it flew into a tropical storm. The first approach was abandoned and a second attempt made several minutes later during which the aircraft descended to a height just above sea level. It hit the sea, bounced and then crashed, over a mile from Gan. The Hastings floated long enough for all 20 persons aboard to evacuate and take to life rafts, from which they were all rescued.

TG580
RAF Gan, Maldives, Indian Ocean, 3rd July 1959. Crashed while landing in a 23 knot crosswind, beyond the aircraft's safety parameters; no diversion or other option however was available to the pilot. The undercarriage was torn off and extensive damage caused to the wings and engines although the fuselage remained intact and none aboard killed. The aircraft, beyond repair, was eventually dragged to and dumped into the sea.

TG583
RAF Dishforth, 31st July 1950. Undershot runway on final approach.

TG584
F
RAF Dishforth, 13th September 1955. Following an attempted overshoot control was lost and the aircraft entered a spin, crashed and possibly caught fire. Five crew members were killed.

TG602
F
RAF Shallufa, Egypt, 12th January 1953. Whilst operating from and flying in the vicinity of Shalluufa this aircraft lost both elevators and crashed killing all nine RAF servicemen on board, 3½ miles from its base. This was one of a number of Hastings sent to support military operations against the Mau-Mau.

TG603
RAF Luqa, Malta, 16th June 1952. Blown off the runway whilst landing in a severe cross wind and subsequently written-off.

TG610
F
RAF Thorney Island, 17th December 1963. Crashed on landing, following which the aircraft carried on and ran into the Radio Servicing Flight workshop at the end of the runway, killing one of the workshop occupants.

TG611
F
Tegel Airport, Berlin, 16th July 1949. Crashed shortly after take-off, the tail trim-tab having been incorrectly set. All five servicemen aboard were killed.

TG613
Mediterranean Sea, 140 miles NW of Benghazi, Libya, 22nd July 1953. En-route to Iraq from Libya via Cyprus with passengers and spare Hercules engines. Three engines failed in succession making a ditching inevitable. All on board escaped the aircraft which sank in just over a minute. All were rescued by a combination of services including RAF Lancaster, USAF SA-16 Albatross and USN P2V Neptune aircraft and a RN destroyer.

TG615
RAF Colerne, 21st October 1957. Whilst attempting an approach and landing the aircraft undershot the runway and bounced. The crew carried-out an overshoot but the Hastings struck a hill a mile away and was damaged beyond repair.

TG624
RAF Aldergrove, 27th December 1961. This was a 202 Squadron MET.1 which, after taking off stalled, crashed-landed and was brought to a stop by raising the undercarriage. Subsequently written-off.

WD478
F
RAF Strubby, Lincolnshire, 19th March 1951. Stalled after take-off and crashed. Three servicemen died and three others survived. This aircraft had been delivered into service on the 13th; six days earlier.

WD483
Ataq airstrip, NE of Aden, 9th April 1956. Undercarriage collapsed when landing and the aircraft caught fire.

WD484
F
Boscombe Down, 2nd March 1955. In use by the RRE this aircraft became airborne with the elevator locks in place, it stalled and crashed killing its two occupants.

WD491
RAF West Raynham, Norfolk. 9th June 1967. One of the main undercarriage wheels failed when landing, the tyre burst and the aircraft was pitched forward onto its nose and came to rest in that position. It was subsequently deemed to be beyond repair and went to RAF Wyton for fire training.

WD492
Greenland, 16th September 1952. Aircraft crashed during 'white out' conditions whilst dropping supplies to members of the British North Greenland Expedition. The aircraft was never recovered.

WD497
F
RAF Seletar, Singapore, 29th May 1961. Whilst conducting a practice supply drop, power from an engine was lost and the aircraft stalled and crashed into the ground, killing all 13 persons on board.

WD498
F
El Adem, Libya, 10th October 1961. During take-off, control was lost and the aircraft crashed back onto the runway. A fire ensued and 17 personnel, mostly Maltese were killed; 20 others survived. It is stated in at least one published source that the pilot's seat had slid back at take-off causing control to be lost!

WJ335
F
RAF Abingdon, 22nd June 1953. Stalled and crashed from approximately 400 feet, killing all six aboard. It was subsequently found that the elevator control locks had been applied or, possibly, never released.

WJ341
RAF Abingdon, 26th July 1955. Undershot runway, ground looped and tore a wing off as a consequence.

WJ342
Eastleigh, Kenya, 23rd January 1961. During take-off an engine failed and the aircraft veered into a grassed area collapsing the undercarriage.

NZ5804
Darwin, Australia, 9th September 1955. Having taken off from RAAF Darwin this aircraft suffered multiple bird strikes, lost power to three engines and made a crash landing as a result of which it was written-off. All 25 occupants survived, even though the aircraft had run into and severed a large diameter water pipe which served the local area.

Appendix V: **A LINGERING FATE AWAITS**

Following retirement the majority of the Hastings fleet was placed into storage, and eventually, after some spares recovery, were offered for sale to scrap merchants and broken up. Some lingered on for several years as ground instructional airframes at various airfields. Both the Fire Fighting and Safety School at Catterick, North Yorkshire, and the Central Training Establishment at Manston, used a few airframes. Several Hastings were also ferried to other airfields for a similar fate. The CAA fire training school at Stansted also used Hastings for this purpose, including the first prototype TE580.

Below: *Hastings MET.1, TG565, No.202 Squadron. This aircraft is finished in the final colour scheme employed by the meteorological Hastings of Coastal Command. TG565 is shown with weather radar fitted which it received for trials purposes in 1963. The motif on the tail fin is of a mallard alighting and formed part of the Squadron badge.*

Centre right: *Hastings MET.1 TG565. It is seen engineless at Shawbury after retirement. This aircraft was struck off charge on 30th November 1966 and is the subject of the illustration above.*

Far right: *Another ex-No.202 Squadron Hastings MET.1, TG572, served with the fire crews at Cosford, and is seen here during 1967.*

Bottom: *After retirement from service with No.242 OCU, TG570 spent its last days with the FF&SS at Catterick for fire training, where it is seen in July 1967. All Adrian Balch*

WD490 formerly with 70 Squadron and named 'Hadrian' served out its final years at RAF Bicester, where it is seen in January 1968. No.70 Squadron was the only RAF unit to name more than one of its Hastings. These included:
C.1s TG509 Hector, TG524 Hercules.
C.2s WD490 Hadrian, WJ328 Horatius and WD486 Helios.
Newark Air Museum

After retirement TG607 was flown to RAF Wildenrath, Germany, for fire practice, and is seen there shortly afterwards with three of its engines removed.
Newark Air Museum

A rare image of TG618 and TG619. Almost all of their working lives were spent at RAE Farnborough and are seen there side by side after retirement in September 1968.
Richard L Ward

MET.1 TG623 at Manston in March 1969. This aircraft had been used for extensive spares recovery, although it has gained a door, presumably from a Transport Command Hastings.
Adrian Balch

This page:

Hastings C.2 WD485 in storage at Shawbury in May 1969, complete with Air Support Command titles and the City of Bath Coat of Arms. Both main wheels have been removed. An Avro Anson C.19 is also visible. via Adrian Balch

Hastings T.5 TG529 at Stansted in June 1969, awaiting its fate with the CAA Fire School. Its H2S dome lies beneath its nose.
Tony Eastwood Collection

Another photograph of TG618 formerly with the MET Flight at RAE Farnborough, in July 1969. Adrian Balch

Bottom left: *Hastings C.1A TG525 spent its last years on a fire dump in Singapore.*
Adrian Balch

Bottom right: *Hastings C.2 WJ337 also served its days out with the Changi fire crews.*
Adrian Balch

Opposite page:

Top: *Hastings C.4, WJ326 still wears its RAF Middle East titles, and was one of many Hastings to end their days at RAF Shawbury.*
via David Tuplin

Centre: *Displaying No.70 Squadron markings, C.1A TG524, Hercules was still clinging to life at Shawbury during late August 1970.*
Adrian Balch

Bottom: *Hastings C.1A TG528 bearing the No.24 Squadron Motif on the tail. Struck off charge in January 1968 this aircraft went to the Skyfame Collection before transferring to IWM Duxford where it currently resides.*
Tony Eastwood Collection

LIST OF ABBREVIATIONS

Back cover: *One of the many roles performed by the Hastings was that of an aircrew trainer for the Royal Air Force V Bomber force during the 1960s and into the 1970s. One example was TG511, seen here landing at an unknown location in the 1970s. One of the last four airworthy Hastings, TG511 now resides within the National Cold War Museum, Cosford.* Adrian Balch Collection

Below: *One of the last two Hastings C.1As to serve with the RAF was TG536 of the SCBS, seen landing at Binbrook on 2nd January 1973. Some parts of this airframe survive today, incorporated into the Halifax rebuild at the Yorkshire Air Museum.* Terry Senior

A&AEE	Aeroplane and Armament Experimental Establishment
AFEE	Airborne Forces Experimental Establishment
ASC	Air Support Command
ASF	Aircraft Servicing Flight
BOAC	British Overseas Airways Corporation
BCBS	Bomber Command Bombing School
C(A)	Controller (Aircraft)
CAA	Civil Aviation Authority
CSE	Central Signals Establishment
CTE	Central Training Establishment
EFS	Empire Flying School
EOKA	National Organisation of Cypriot Fighters
ETPS	Empire Test Flying School
FCRT	Fire and Crash Rescue Training
FEAF	Far East Air Force
FECS	Far East Communications Squadron
FF&SS	Fire Fighting and Safety School
GAL	General Aircraft Limited
GIA	Ground Instructional Airframe
HP	Handley Page
IRIS	International Radio Installations and Systems
IWM	Imperial War Museum
MAP	Ministry of Aircraft Production
MEAF	Middle East Air Force
MECS	Middle East Communications Squadron
MET	Meteorological
MOS	Ministry of Supply
MOTAT	Museum of Transport and Technology

MRF	Meteorological Research Flight
MU	Maintenance Unit
NACA	National Advisory Council of Aeronautics
NEAF	Near East Air Force
OCU	Operational Conversion Unit
OUT	Operational Training Unit
PTS	Parachute Training School
PTU	Parachute Training Unit
RAE	Royal Aircraft Establishment
RAF	Royal Air Force
RAFFC	Royal Air Force Flying College
RNZAF	Royal New Zealand Air Force
RRE	Royal Radar Establishment
RRF	Radar Reconnaissance Flight
SAS	Special Air Service
SBAC	Society of British Aerospace Companies
SCBS	Strike Command Bombing School
SOC	Struck Off Charge
SOE	Special Operations Executive
TCASF	Transport Command Airborne Support Flight
TCDF	Transport Command Development Flight
TCDU	Transport Command Development Unit
TRE	Telecommunication Research Establishment
USA	United States of America
VIP	Very Important Person
WEE	Winterisation Experimental Establishment
WFU	Withdrawn From Use
W/O	Written Off